ALCOHOL AND DRUG USE
IN NEPAL

WITH REFERENCE TO CHILDREN

By

Rupa Dhital
Govind Subedi
Yogendra B Gurung
Prabha Hamal

May, 200

CWIN
Child Workers in Nepal Concerned Centre (CWIN)

ii

Study Team

Co-ordinator:	Rupa Dhital
Contributors:	Govind Subedi, Yogendra B Gurung, Prabha Hamal
Advisors:	Ibrahima Thioub, Dr. Om Gurung
Assistants:	Bal Bahadur Rai, Raju Maharjan, Ram Chandra Shai, Sri Ram Mishra and Tulsi Rijal
Interviewers:	Chet Kumari Gurung, Kamala Rai, Dinesh Gurung, Ganga Subedi, Sher Bahadur Shrestha, Raj Kumar Gurung, Januka Tamang, Usha Maharjan, Tulsi Baral, Raj Kumar Yadav, Deepen Gurung, Bharat Ghimire, Nav Raj Tamang, and Narendra Gurung

First published:	May, 2001
Printed at:	Kantipur Offset Press, Kathmandu, Nepal.
Published by:	Child Workers in Nepal Concerned Centre (CWIN)
	P.O. Box 4374, Kathmandu, Nepal
	Tel: (977 1) 282255, 278064
	Fax: (977 1) 278016
	E-mail: cwin@mos.com.np
	Web Site: http://www.cwin-nepal.org
ISBN:	99933-343-0-8
Price:	Rs. 200.00

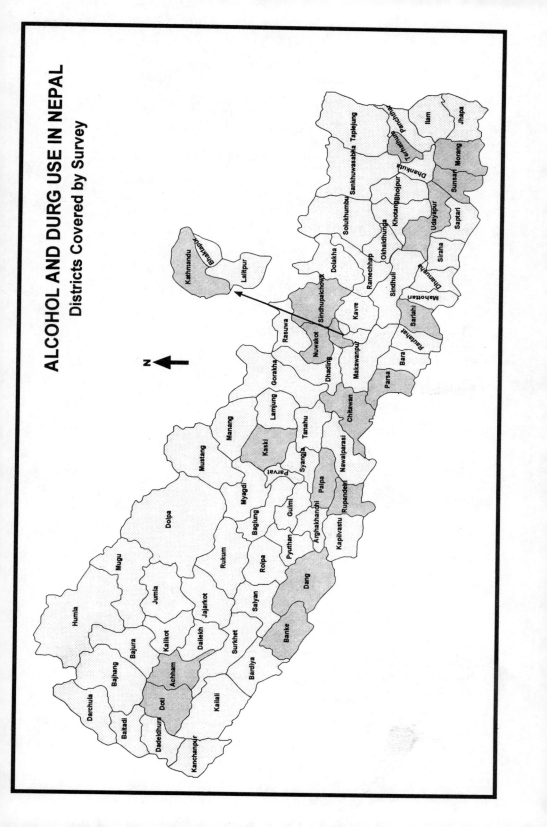

ALCOHOL AND DURG USE IN NEPAL
Districts Covered by Survey

TABLE OF CONTENTS

Chapter VI: Impact of Alcohol Use on Children's Lives

Chapter VII: Counter-forces for the Prevention of Alcohol, Drugs, and Tobacco Use

Chapter VIII: Summary and Conclusions

Acknowledgements

Many people have contributed to make this study possible. Lajla Blom, Social Scientist from Norway and the former International Coordinator of Local Action, FORUT who initiated the whole process of knowledge based project in Nepal and thus sow the first seed for this research. Ibrahima Thioub, Historian from University of Dakar, Senegal, and current International Coordinator of Local Action, FORUT provided his assistance throughout the survey. I am grateful to them.

I am thankful to CWIN for the opportunity to coordinate this study for Local Action and to FORUT, Norway for financial and other support. Thanks are also due to other colleagues at CWIN who created information documentation crucial for the research, and to the children at the CWIN centres who provided the preliminary information that contributed in gaining insight to further study with other groups of children.

I am grateful to Dr. Om Gurung, Anthropologist, for his valuable advises, and Dr. Bal Kumar KC, Professor, Tribhuvan University, Nepal, for bringing this report in the publishable form.

Research assistants (Bal Bahadur Rai, Tulsi Rijal, Shri Ram Mishra, Ram Kumar Shahi and Raju Maharjan) and interviewers (Chet Kumari Gurung, Kamala Rai, Dinesh Gurung, Ganga Subedi, Sher Bahadur Shrestha, Raj Kumar Gurung, Januka Tamang, Usha Maharjan, Tulsi Baral, Raj Kumar Yadav, Deepen Gurung, Bharat Ghimire, Nav Raj Tamang, and Narendra Gurung) deserve special thanks for their contribution to this work.

Thanks are also due to individuals, organisations, and local government representatives in the community who accepted to be the key informants. And to the respondents in research area across Nepal - children, women, men - all of whom made this study possible.

Rupa Dhital
Coordinator, Local Action - CWIN

Foreword

This study was undertaken by Child Workers in Nepal Concerned Centre (CWIN) in 2000 in order to generate basic knowledge on the use of alcohol and drug by the people of Nepal with reference to children. This study was a major activity of Local Action, a joint project between CWIN and FORUT (Campaign for Development and Solidarity) which is a Norway based NGO that is engaged in development cooperation in Sri Lanka, India, Senegal, The Gambia, Sierra Leone and Nepal. Local Action was designed in FORUT as an international project with an aim to strengthen counter-forces against the culture of alcohol and drug use locally.

CWIN, established in 1987, is a pioneer organisation in Nepal for the rights of the child and against child labour exploitation. It is an advocate organisation for child rights with focus on child labour, street children, child abuse, trafficking in children and other related issues. CWIN acts as children's voice lobbying, campaigning and pressurizing the government to protect and promote children's rights in the country, and to end all kinds of exploitation, abuse and discrimination against children in its different local and national programmemes. Alcohol and other drug use have been internalised by CWIN as an important and necessary component in its work with children. In order to design an effective prevention programmeme, an acute need was felt to identify the real extent of alcohol and drug use in cultural, economic and social context. A study comprising such perspectives that looked into the impact of alcohol and drug use on children was lacking in Nepal.

This is the first comprehensive national study covering about 2,400 households in 16 districts representing both rural and urban areas as well as all ecological and development regions in Nepal. Most study so far provide little and fragmentary information on the use of alcohol and drugs. This study departs from other studies in four ways. First, it provides baseline information on the use of alcohol, tobacco and other drugs across different strata of population. Second, it aims to understand the extent, context and patterns of consumption. Thirdly, it examines the impact of the use of alcohol and drug on children's lives including the level of children's own initiation and consumption. Finally, it intends to identify social counterforces and intervention strategies to reduce and prevent harmful use of alcohol and other drugs.

We argue that being a multicultural and mutli-ethnic country, Nepal is largely ambivalent society regarding alcohol use. With the passage of time, traditional sanctions and caste-bound censors have disappeared. The use of alcohol and drug affects all strata of society. The alcohol industry is powerful and enjoys a stronghold on national economy generating one of the highest revenues. The alcohol policies are conducive to market, and alcohol is available everywhere and to all age-groups without any restriction. The same is true for tobacco. Drugs are strictly illegal in Nepal but are prevalent into the market through different channels. The easy access and availability of drugs and alcohol has created an extremely conducive social environment for people to initiate substance use, specially among young people and children. The anti-alcohol movements started by women's groups resulting in dry-zones and prohibited areas, though enjoyed initial success, have not been sustainable due to market pressure and lack of legal standing. In this background, the Local Action was integrated in CWIN in 1999 as a knowledge based project aiming at prevention of the use of alcohol and drug through social action.

In Nepal, a need for comprehensive policy and programme has been felt to effectively address the situation of alcohol and drug consumption in the country. The findings of this study may be useful in designing prevention programmes, both targeted at adults and children. While creating a base-line data, many issues have emerged that could be taken up by further research in order to build on the understanding of alcohol and drug dynamics in our society. Finally, it is hoped that the study will shed light on the issues of alcohol and drug consumption to the government and civil society alike.

I would like to congratulate the study team for a successful undertaking, and extend thanks to everyone who contributed to this study.

Gauri Pradhan
President, CWIN

Chapter I

Introduction

Nepal is a multi-ethnic, multi cultural, multi religious and multi linguistic society with a rich repertoire of customs and traditions. It is also a geographically diverse country and a caste bound society. The 1991 population census identified a total of 60 caste/ethnic groups in the country, with 29 in Tarai, 29 in hills and 2 in the mountain as their origin. Nepal is an officially Hindu country with the constitutional provision of no discrimination against any other religion. Hinduism is practiced by over 86 per cent of the population, followed by Buddhism (7.8%) and Islam (3.5%). There are also other religions like Kirant, Jain, Christian and others. Historically, various religious and cultural groups practiced alcohol in Nepal.

1.1 History of Alcohol in Nepal

From ancient times, Nepal has been a common ground of people from both Indo-Aryan and Tibeto-Mangoloid races. It has also achieved a remarkable compromise between Hinduism and Buddhism with divergent values system (Britannica.com 1999-2001). Social, religious, cultural values which governed food habits, customs and beliefs of people have been fundamental in governing the Nepali civilization over different periods of history (Adhikari, 1988 cited in Subedi, 1999).

All cultures possess a set of ideal attitudes toward the consumption of, or abstention from alcoholic beverages, and define the expected and prohibited behaviour while drinking (Mohan and Sharma, 1995). Four cultural settings have been conceptualised in relation to alcohol use. First, abstinent cultures which condemn the use of alcoholic beverages in any form, such as Muslims and ascetic Protestants. Second, ambivalent cultures, in which sternly negative and prohibitive attitudes coexist and idealizing intoxication such as in the English-speaking and Scandinavian nations. Third, permissive cultures such as Jews and Italians, which tolerate moderate consumption but condemn excessive drinking. Finally, overly permissive cultures, in which the prevalent attitude is permissive toward drinking alcohol, and drunkenness is generally accepted in certain contexts as among the French and the Japanese.

In Nepal, the drinking culture probably fits into the second model where abstinence and permissiveness towards drinking co-exists.

Alcohol use is closely related with the caste system of Nepal[1]. Many people foster the use of alcohol beverage according to their social, religious and cultural traditions. The people of Mangoloid origin used alcohol for the purpose of rituals and on religious occasion, as well as for social drinking during festivals and special occasion like birth and death. On the other hand, the Hindu society, based on the code of Manu, prohibited alcohol use among the higher caste of Brahmin and Chhetri. The societal structure laid out by the semi-legendary lawgiver Manu about 200 BC set strict rules for societal behaviour and hierarchy (Mohan and Sharma, 1995). Despite attempts at reform from time to time, his influence has persisted and still strongly governs rural, and to a lesser extent urban life. Manu's classification into *vernas* (caste) has survived. The code of Manu strongly prohibits alcohol use among the so-called priest caste *Brahmins* (Subedi, 1999). It also prohibits drinking for *Chhettri* (warrier) and *Baishya* (traders). While the *sudra* (working caste) could drink according to their custom.

The alcohol practice seems to have a long history in Nepal. Pivotal evidence suggests that even in pre-historic and ancient times alcohol was consumed. Traditional use of alcohol in the rituals, cultural and social events persisted among Kirats. While the surviving Liccahvi inscription does not reveal much about the use of beverages, it can be

---

[1] The division of Nepalese society in different hierarchical caste system was based on the code of Manu. King Jayasthiti Malla (1382-1395 AD) of Kathmandu first decreed the law that stratified the whole Nepali society based on division of *Tagadhari* (Brahmin, Chetri and Thakuri) and *Matwali* (Tharus, Gurings, Tamangs, Newars, Rais, Limbus, Sherpas, Jirels, Sunuwars and others). The former group was not permitted to use alcohol while the latter was (Subba et al., 1995).

assumed that alcohol use continued among the lower strata of the caste system and among the indigenous people such as Kirants and Newars.

In the middle period, Newars adopted and followed the Trantrism- a sect of Hindusim which emphasized Matsya (fish), Mamsha (meat) and Madira (alcohol) among food items even during the rituals (Vaidya, et al., 1993). The Newars made variety of alcoholic beverages from rice, fruits and millets. The medieval inscription mentions a variety of beers (*Kalathwan, Ajithwan, Katathwan, Karithawan, Kejulithwan, Hyaunthwan*) and *Ayela* (spirit), then popular drinks among Newars.

Some historians also linked the loss of territory in Nepalese history as the result of excessive use of alcohol. Prithivi Narayan Shaha, the King of Gorkha, strategically chose the day of Indra Jatra (25 September), a local festival, to attack the drunk Kathmanduits, chiefly alcohol using Newar ethnic group and succeeded in his effort (Sharma, 1976 cited in Subedi 1999). His successor introduced the first civil code of Nepal in AD 1854 based on Hindu doctrine and marginalised the Matwalis till the early years of 1960s (Subba et al., 1995). Only the modern and amended civil code of 1962 did away with discrimination based on caste that included separate punishments for those belonging to higher and lower castes while caught drinking alcohol.

It is argued that after 1850, the use of foreign alcohol among ruling elite has started in Nepal. Janga Bahadur Rana, the then Prime Minister of Nepal, visited England in 1850. He and his entourage that followed him to his European travel seemed to have developed the taste and introduced alcohol among the rich and powerful nobles of Nepal who were erstwhile strict followers of Hinduism. After that, western alcohol beverages like White Horse and Black Horse became internalised in the palaces (Vaidya et al., 1993).

"Jang Bahadur's son enjoyed drinking wines and spirits and imported alcoholic drinks in large quantities... Almost every evening the young sons of the Prime Minister (Jang) hosted drinks and dinner parties in their homes. The invitees very willingly joined the parties and drank freely... Every alcohol drink was then classified as wine in Rana houses. But the most popular drinks were John Exshaw No 1

Cognac and French and Portuguese red wine. They often drank straight and consumed several bottles in one sitting. Some of the young ladies were also addicted to alcoholic drinks (Rana,1978 cited in Vaidya et al., 1993)."

The evidence of alcohol use among elite in Kathmandu is also evident from Daniel Wright's writing (1958): "The higher classes are supposed not to touch spirits, as they would lose caste by doing so. Strange to say, however, no trade is so profitable in Nepal as that of important brandy or champagne."

Further influence in drinking patterns are seen as being imported through several developments that marked the general people's access to outside world. Some historians argue that Nepali soldiers recruited in the British Army were sent to suppress 1857 Mutiny in India. These Nepalese soldiers who were involved in First World War (1914-18) and the Second World War (1939-44) were the main agents to popularize western drinking habits in the society (Subedi, 1999; Shah, 2000). Similarly, the process of home production of alcohol for sale and establishments of *bhatti* (traditional pubs) in both rural and urban settings probably took root after 1918 when the soldiers returned with cash, new desires and consumerist culture. Before that the Nepali society had not been monetised and there was no alcohol trade. Similarly, those employed in India, Burma (Myanmar), Malaya (Singapore and Malaysia) and the elite who had the opportunity to get modern education abroad influenced social acceptance of drinking. This way, it can be seen that while the society was transforming itself from traditional to modern age with the introduction of modern education and exposure to outside world, the drinking pattern became elitists in the mode of western culture. Gradually, the rapid socialisation and acceptance of drinking in society took place while the traditional values and norm began to erode gradually.

The industrial production of alcoholic beverages started after the 1960s. The pioneer alcohol producers in the country, namely Mahendra Sugar Mills and Jawalakhel Distillery were reported as being established in 1963 and 1972 respectively. As an extremely profitable industry, alcohol industry began to expand rapidly and the consumerist culture was established. The alcohol culture received another boost after the democratic movement of 1989 where liberal policies gave alcohol industry a conducive environment to foster.

1.2 Alcohol and Drug Use in the Present Context

At present, social tolerance to alcohol use is quite high. Production, sale and consumption of alcohol is ever on the increase and it could be taken as the number one problem substance abuse in the country (Shrestha, 1992 cited in Biswas et al., 2000). Consumption of alcohol is prevalent among almost all-ethnic groups irrespective of the caste hierarchy. Traditionally the whole Nepalese society is segmented on the basis of alcohol use. *Matwali* are traditional alcohol users, and *Tagadharis* are traditional alcohol non-users. Most ethnic groups and 'untouchables' - the lower strata of Hindu hierarchical caste system- are the traditionally alcohol users. Whereas Brahmin, Chhetri and Thakuri - the higher strata of the Hindu hierarchical caste system- are considered as traditional alcohol non-users. However, the cultural barriers for the consumption of alcohol have almost disappeared and there are a few cultural groups where alcohol has not been used. It is estimated that almost one-half of the Nepalese population consumes alcohol. The most likely groups are the younger generations, especially males, in traditional non-user groups. A WHO study (Internet: http://www.who.int/toh) indicates that early onset and continued use of illicit substances is more likely to occur among young people from communities with poor social and economic performance. Family drinking, drinking environment, availability and accessibility, socio-psychological circumstances and alcohol image are considered as contributing factors for alcohol use among young people in Nepal (Dhital, 1999). Children learn to drink alcohol in the family at young ages. They use alcohol in the family as part of food and during several occasions.

Use of alcohol is not only a culture but also a problem when it becomes excessive. Excessive or uncontrolled drinking of alcohol may damage children's health, psychology, and ultimately lives. Dhital (1999) noted that children are exposed to several problems like violence in family, aggression, disgrace, self-hurt, involvement in offensive action and illness. In addition, children of alcoholics are found to show less social competency, more internalising and externalising behaviours, more negative activity, lower academic achievement and more psychiatric distress (Sinha et al., 2000).

In addition to alcohol, other types of drug use also exist in Nepal, such as cannabis (*Ganja*), synthetic drugs and tobacco. Consumption of cannabis is connected with Hindu religion, as one of the favourite substance of *Lord Shiva*. Cannabis is an indigenous plant in Nepal. It is age-old. Cannabis is illicitly cultivated and grown in high hills of mid-west, central and far-western part of Nepal. In Tarai, its illicit cultivation is common (Spotlight, March 2000). Cannabis seems to have been sub-culturally acceptable.

Drug use began to be seen as a problem in the country for the first time the mid 1960s and early 1970s with the influx of large number of hippies [Ministry of Home Affairs (MOH), 1998]. Heroin use was in an epidemic form in Nepal from 1980s onwards. Since early 1990s, psychotropic drugs have been widely used by the drug users in Nepal.

It is found that 0.5 to 1 per cent of the population in the Tarai use cannabis on a daily basis (MOH, 1996). The MOH (1998) estimated that there were more than 50,000 drug users in Nepal excluding those using cannabis, alcohol and tobacco. Majority constituted of young people of 15-30 years. These young people come from all kinds of social, economic, religious and ethnic backgrounds with different reasons for taking drugs. Cannabis, heroin, opiates, tranquilisers and methaqualone are the most common drugs available in the country. Apart from tobacco and alcohol, according to Chatterjee et al. (1996), the major drugs abused in Nepal were cannabis, and codeine containing cough syrup, nitrazepam tablets, and buprenor-phine injections. Heroin is the second most prevalent drug in the country. It is estimated that more than 25,000 people in Nepal is dependent on heroin. Its major concentration is reported to be in the Kathmandu and Pokhara valleys and Dharan. The cultivation of opium is limited in Nepal. Methaqualone is the newly introduced drug in the market. However, the consumption of opium and its derivatives are found to be decreasing among the drug users but the use of pharmaceutical drugs is increasing in an alarming rate (MOH, 1999). Increased use of psychotropic drugs is due to its easy availability and low price.

The problems of drug abuse are localised especially in the urban, semi-urban areas and along the border of Nepal and India. Most of the drug addicts are found in Kathmandu, Lalitpur, Pokhara, Biratanagar, Dharan, Birgunj, Nepalgunj and Bhairahawa. The Drug Abuse

Prevention Association of Nepal (DAPAN) in its 1990 survey of the high school and campuses in Kathmandu, Pokhara and Biratanagar found that 32.4 per cent of the students had tried different types of drugs. A large number of addicts had used psychotropic substances. About 2.5 per cent of the students had used heroin and 2.5 per cent tried opium at least once (The Rising Nepal, 15 May, 1996).

Unlike other drugs, tobacco production and consumption is common in Nepal. About 7,300 hectares of land were harvested for tobacco accounting for 0.3 per cent of all arable land in Nepal (WHO, 1990). Production of tobacco is also substantial, approximately 6,580 million cigarettes is produced annually. This accounts for around 0.12 per cent of the world's tobacco production.

Tobacco industry has also become one of the major employment generating industries in Nepal. It provides employment to more than 10,000 people. In 1990, more than half of the total government revenue from industry came from tobacco taxes. Over 90 per cent of the industrial taxes from tobacco are paid by cigarette companies, with the rest coming from *Bidi* manufacturers. In the early 1990s, per capita consumption of cigarettes among population (aged 15 years and above) averaged 580, up from about 290 in the early 1980s. The chewing types of tobacco are commonly knows as 'Khaini', 'Panparag', 'Gutkha', and 'Jarda'.

Most studies so far conducted in Nepal provide little or no information on the use of alcohol and drugs. They are largely based on targeted groups or on hospital records. They do not provide the information on the alcohol and drugs behaviour in different strata of population. This study departs from other studies in four ways. First, it provides the baseline information on alcohol and drugs use for different strata of population. Second, it aims to understand the societal aspect of alcohol and drug use. Third, it examines the impact of alcohol use on children's life. Finally, it intends to provide social counter forces and intervention strategies to reduce and prevent harmful use of alcohol and drugs.

Chapter II

Methods and Materials

2.1 Selection of Study Areas

Study areas were selected in five stages. In the first stage, 16 out of 75 districts were selected based on following criteria:

- Administrative regions (east, central, west, mid west and far west)
- Geographical region (hill, mountain, tarai)
- Ethnic composition
- Place of residence (rural and urban)
- Origin of street children

At the second stage, 10 VDCs and 6 urban centres were selected considering major ethnic clusters and the magnitude of street children.

At the third stage, three wards from each VDC/urban centre were drawn at random. Fifty households within each selected ward were selected through systematic random sampling. If the ward did not have 50 households, additional households from adjoining ward were interviewed. Finally, 10 out of 50 households (or every fifth household) were selected as a sub-sample of the main survey for the interview of children using systematic random sampling technique.

2.2 Sample Size and Target Population

The target population of the study were as follows:

- adult member of the household from all sampled households
- children aged 10-17 years from every fifth household from the main survey

The total number of clusters surveyed was 48 (16 sampling areas in 3 clusters). Thirty clusters were from rural areas and 18 were from urban areas (Table 2.1). This provided a total of 2,400 households (50

Table 2.1 Selection of the sample and its criteria

Districts	Municipality (U=Urban)	Regions	Major Ethnic Cluster	Sample Size			
				Adults		Children	
				Expected no.of households	Total no.of household surveyed	Expected to be inter-viewed	Total Inter-viewed
Terhathum	Basantpur	Eastern-hill	Limbu	150	149	30	30
Sunsari	Dharan (U)	Eastern-Tarai	Rai/Limbu	150	146	30	30
Morang	Urlabari	Eastern-Tarai	Dhimal	150	150	30	25
Udaypur	Rauta	Eastern – Tarai	Rai/Magar	150	147	30	29
Sarlahi	Sisautia	Central-Tarai	Tarai origin	150	143	30	29
Parsa	Brigunj (U)	Central-Tarai	Muslim/Yadav	150	143	30	26
Chitwan	Bharatpur (U)	Central-Tarai	Mixed	150	141	30	20
Kathmandu	Kathmandu (U)	Central-hills	Newar	150	147	30	29
Nuwakot	Chaturale	Central-hills	Tamang	150	147	30	29
Sindhupalchowk	Talamarang	Central-mount	Mixed	150	147	30	34
Kaski	Pokhara (U)	Western hills	Gurung	150	143	30	21
Palpa	Rupse	Western hills	Magar	150	145	30	19
Ruppandehi	Tikuligadi	Western Tarai	Mixed	150	147	30	22
Dang	Lalmatiya	Mid-western Tarai	Tharu	150	139	30	30
Banke	Nepalgunj (U)	Mid-western Tarai	Muslim	150	150	30	27
Doti	Mudabara	Far-west hills	Chettri/Thakuri	150	149	30	26
			Total	2,400	2,333	480	426

households in 48 clusters). The total sample included 1800 households from rural areas and 600 from urban areas. A total of 2,333 households were successfully interviewed with an overall response rate of 97.2 per cent.

The number of clusters for interviewing children was 30 from rural and 18 from urban areas. Thus, the expected number of interviews was 480 with 10 children from each cluster. Altogether 426 children were successfully interviewed with a response rate of 89 per cent. A relatively high non-response rate resulted due to children's absence from home during the survey.

2.3 Instruments for Data Collection

Two types of instruments were applied to collect information related to the objectives of the study. Quantitative information was obtained from household survey (household and individual questionnaire). Qualitative information was obtained through case studies and key informant interviews.

2.3.1 Household Survey

Three sets of questionnaire were administered: household schedule and two sets of individual questionnaire, one for adults and another for children aged 10-17 years.

i. Household Schedule

The purpose of household schedule is to obtain data on socio-economic and demographic characteristics of the sample population such as age, sex, educational attainment, and marital status, occupation, and place of residence, caste/ethnicity and religion and practice of alcohol, drugs and tobacco. This information is important to estimate the prevalence of the use of alcohol, drug and tobacco among respondents by gender, age, education, occupational status, caste/ethnicity, and place of residence. Household schedule also provides information on alcohol production, sale and consumption.

ii. Individual Questionnaire for Adults

An adult member was selected from the sampled household for the detail information on the socio-cultural/ religious meanings and roles, frequency, patterns and context of alcohol/drugs/tobacco use by gender, age, rural/urban and by different social strata. It also provides information on perception on alcohol and/or drug consumption .

iii. Questionnaire for Children Aged 10-17

The study targeted different groups of children - literate/illiterate, urban/rural, working/non-working, traditional user and non-user group and different social and family backgrounds. The main purpose of the schedule was to understand the impact of household alcohol/drug use on children's lives; settings, environment, cultural orientations and other factors influencing their own initiative to drinking/using drugs.

2.3.2 Qualitative Information: Key Informant Interviews and Case Studies

Key informants were those who are knowledgeable about the issue of alcohol and drugs. They are:

- Community leaders,
- Local government/administration,
- School teachers,
- Health personnel,
- Alcohol entrepreneurs,
- NGOs/CBOs/Women's organisations,
- Police, and
- Anti-alcohol/drug activists.

One respondent from each cluster representing different gender, ethnicity, age, place of residence and social status was interviewed for an in-depth information.

2.4 Data Collection

Field operation was conducted during January and February, 2000. At the central level, five research associates and 15 enumerators with at least Intermediate level of education were appointed. They were trained with social activists and professionals with experience in alcohol, drugs and related issues among children.

A ten-day training was held for supervisors and enumerators. The focus of the training was to share knowledge on alcohol, drugs and tobacco. They were also instructed on how to ensure the accuracy of the responses. Research team closely supervised the field work.

2.5 Methodological Issues

Given the diversity of the Nepalese population on the use of alcohol, drugs and tobacco, this study has covered samples from rural and urban areas, ecological zones, development regions and major ethnic groups of Nepal. A total of 16 out of 75 districts were covered to provide the estimates of the prevalence rate of alcohol, drugs and tobacco at the national level.

One problem encountered in fixing the sample size was the differences in prevalence rates of alcohol, drugs and tobacco use. Whereas the alcohol was common in some caste and ethnic groups of Nepal, for others it is a socio-cultural taboo. Drug use is a completely illegal affair. In case of tobacco, it is commonly used across the population. Had there been a larger sample size, there would have been greater precision of the estimates of drug use at the household level.

2.6 Ethical Issues Encountered in the Survey

One of the ethical issues of the survey was to come across the segmented Nepalese society along the lines of alcohol user and non-user. Researchers faced problems/dilemmas how to handle this issue. It was difficult to approach a household where traditionally alcohol use is not allowed. There was a particular gender related problem when a woman was a respondent. In Nepal, women are reluctant to report about their husband's drinking habit in front of a stranger.

In case of children's interviews, some people frequently interrupted our research team saying "why do you people ask these questions to such an immature family members?" Among non-user families, people also objected to questions about alcohol, which was inappropriate. Children were often reluctant to report their drinking behaviour in front of both strangers and adult family members.

In case of drug use, respondents were much reluctant to report about themselves but were quite forthcoming in reporting drug use by neighbours.

2.7 Assurance of Quality of Data

Maximum efforts were made to ensure the quality of data. First, research assistants and enumerators were given a ten-day rigorous training. Second, WHO questionnaires were utilised and pre-tested in the cultural context of Nepal. Third, questionnaire was designed in such a way that sequence of the events could be easily captured. Fourth, some of the attitude questions were probed and filtered. Fifth, data were edited in the field. If there was a serious error, enumerators were instructed to revisit the respondents. Sixth, the researchers supervised and monitored the fieldwork. Finally, data were again edited during the computer entry.

2.8 Limitation of the Study

This study is the first knowledge-based of its kind. There are no studies conducted on this topic by a reasonably large sample size.

The information was collected by purposive sampling method while selecting area but systematic random sampling while selecting households. So, caution should be taken in generalising the results.

Even though this study covers three substances (alcohol, drugs, and tobacco) at the same time, the focus of the study was on alcohol. Therefore, a detail analysis on the use of drugs and tobacco is not carried out.

2.9 Organisation of the Study

This study is divided into eight chapters. The first chapter introduces the study and explores a brief historical legacy on the use of alcohol and drugs. The second chapter includes procedure of the study in selecting target population for interviews. The third chapter describes the characteristics of the sample population by different socio-economic and demographic characteristics. Chapter four deals with the alcohol economy at national and household levels. Chapter five deals with the sociability of alcohol, drugs, and tobacco with respect to the extent, patterns, contexts, and attitude and perceptions. Chapter six assesses the impact of alcohol use on children's lives. Chapter seven examines the counter-forces related to alcohol and drugs use. The final chapter summarizes and concludes the findings and recommends suggestions for further research.

Chapter III

Socio-economic and Demographic Characteristics of Sample Population

3.1 Demographic Characteristics of the Sample Population

The total sample population comprised of 13,526 persons in 2,333 households with a sex ratio of 110.6 males per 100 females. This high sex ratio compared to the national sex ratio of 101 may be due to underreporting of those males who out-migrated from the household for 6 months or more. More than one third of the sample population consisted of child population aged under 15 years and 41 in 100 persons were children aged under 18 years (Table 3.1).

Table 3.1 Age Distribution of the Household Population

Age Group	Cumulative Per cent	N
Under 18	41.2	5,581
18-64	54.7	7,492
65 & above	5.0	546
Total		13,526
Sex ratio		110.6

3.2 Socio-economic Characteristics of the Sample Population

This study obtained information on caste/ethnicity, traditional status of alcohol users or non-users of the sample population. Altogether 42 types of ethnic groups were identified in the sample. These were classified into 6 groups based on the caste and ethnic divisions recommended by His Majesty Government of Nepal (Appendix 1). Hill high caste accounted for 37.2 per cent, hill low cast for 7.6, and

Tarai caste for 8.1 per cent of the total household population. The sample population is also categorized along the line of traditional alcohol users and non-users (Appendix 2). In this study, traditional users accounted for 54.3 per cent and the non-users accounted for 45 per cent.

Table 3.2 Socio-cultural Characteristics of the Sample Population

Background characteristics	Per cent	N
Caste/ethnicity[1]		
Hill high caste	37.2	5,032
Hill low caste	7.6	1,033
Hill ethnic group	33.2	4,497
Tarai caste	8.1	1,095
Tarai ethnic group	10.1	1,364
Others	3.7	505
Traditional status of alcohol use		
Traditional user	54.3	7,345
Traditional non-user	44.9	6,079
Unspecified	0.8	102
Total	100.0	13,526

Table 3.3 displays the socio-economic contexts of the sample population. The overall literacy rate is 70.6 per cent, which is much higher than the national average of 40 per cent in 1991. The high literacy level compared to national level may be due to expansion of non-formal education and the effect of modernization in the rural areas. People are implicitly exposed to urban and modernity due to rapid expansion of NGOs and INGOs activities. Consequently, even though people are illiterate, they do not tend to report themselves as illiterate. This tendency exaggerates the literacy level. Of the literate, majority have completed primary level of education (35.3%). This is followed by those completed secondary (29.5%) and then by those having SLC and above (21%) level of education. Majority of household population are found to be in agriculture (60%).

---

[1] Considering the hierarchical caste system, hill caste has been divided into two groups: hill high caste, hill low caste. There is also hierarchical caste system among Tarai populations but they are not desegregated.

Table 3.3 Education and Occupation of the Sample Population

Education/Occupation	Per cent	N
Educational Status (6 years+)		
Literate	70.6	8,309
No Schooling	14.3	1,191
Primary	35.3	2,929
Secondary	29.5	2,452
SLC	10.2	846
Intermediate	6.6	548
Bachelor & above	4.1	343
Occupation (10 years+)		
Agriculture	60.0	7,759
Non-agriculture	16.3	1,914
Household work	17.8	2,097
Total	100.0	11,770

3.3 Livelihood Strategies of the Households

Respondents were asked their three major sources of livelihood. Producing and selling of alcohol is not the primary or secondary source of income for their livelihood (Table 3.4).

Economic activities such as agriculture, business traditional occupation like shoe making, tailoring, iron and gold-smith, government service, and cottage industry appear to be the primary sources of income for the livelihood. Similarly, house-rent, agriculture rented in, non-governmental service, agriculture wage labour, wage labour, and domestic servant are reported to be the secondary sources of income.

Table 3.4 Main Sources of Livelihood for Households

Activities	Sources of livelihood			
	Primary	Secondary	Tertiary	N
1. Agriculture (own)	81.3	14.8	3.9	1,526
2. Shop/Hotel/Restaurant	65.4	27.7	6.9	462
3. Traditional occupation*	54.2	36.1	9.6	83
4. Govt. service	51.9	44.5	3.6	443
5. Cottage industry	38.3	32.5	29.2	209
6. House rent	21.3	62.3	16.3	239
7. Tenant farming	30.6	56.7	12.8	180
8. Non-Govt. service	36.7	54.9	8.5	390
9. Agri wage labour	30.2	54.6	15.3	295
10. Wage labour	20.7	51.1	28.2	479
11. Domestic servant	19.6	41.3	39.1	46
12. Porter	5.4	46.4	48.2	56
13. Alcohol production/sale	11.5	43.8	44.8	96

* *Traditional occupation includes tailoring (Damai), iron/gold-smithing (Lohar/sunar), and shoe-making (Sarki).*

Respondents were further asked whether they have had sufficient food around the year from their three major sources of income. One-fifth of respondents lacked food sufficiency around the year (Table 3.5). Majority of them were from mountain and hill (22.3%), from rural areas (28.2%), and of traditional alcohol user group (24.1%).

Table 3.5 Economic sufficiency for the family

Background characteristics	Sufficient	Insufficient	N
Place of Residence			
Rural	71.8	28.2	1,437
Urban	96.8	3.2	844
Ecological zone			
Mountain/Hill	77.7	22.3	1,011
Kathmandu	100.0	-	146
Tarai	81.6	18.4	1,124
Traditional status of alcohol use			
Traditional user	75.9	24.1	1,242
Traditional non-user	87.3	12.7	1,022
Unspecified	82.4	17.6	17
Total	81.1	18.9	2,281

Of the respondents with difficulty to support themselves around the year, 3 in 10 reported to insufficient livelihood for at least 6 months and 8 in 10 lacked livelihood for at least nine months from their major sources of income. The pattern is similar among rural residents, whereas the per cent of those who think their main source of income as insufficient for livelihood is relatively less in urban areas than in rural areas (Table 3.6).

Table 3.6 Livelihood Pattern Among Those Who Do Not Survive a Year

Livelihood sufficiency	Rural		Urban		Total	
	%	Cum. %	%	Cum. %	%	Cum. %
For <3 months	7.2	7.2	7.4	7.4	7.2	7.2
3-5 months	22.2	29.4	14.8	22.2	21.8	29.0
6-8 months	52.3	81.7	55.6	77.8	52.5	81.5
9-12 months	18.3	100.0	22.2	100.0	18.5	100.0
N	(405)	-	(27)	-	(432)	-

In such a context of poverty, alcohol becomes a major source of economic support in some poorest of the poor households and contributes to Government revenue, which will be dealt in the following chapter.

Chapter IV

Alcohol Economy in Nepal

This chapter explores the role of alcohol in Nepalese economy both at the local and national levels. Utilising the secondary data from the Ministry of Industry and Department of VAT, Ministry of Finance, role of alcohol at national economy is examined. Similarly, the role of alcohol economy at local level is examined through the household level information collected in the field.

4.1 Alcohol Economy at the National Level

The industrialisation of alcohol in Nepal started during the early 1970s and it is on the rise over the years. If one is to look at the graph of industrial development over the last 10 years, it is probably the alcohol industry that occupies the most prominent place along with the tobacco industry. There is a massive import of liquors from abroad and the production of alcohol takes place from multinational industries operating in Nepal. The industry manufactures liquors from distilleries and breweries, and some home brewed and distilled liquors find the way to market. There are about a dozen brands of beer, and several brands of whiskey, vodka, rum and scotch that are produced in Nepal. Among them, all beers and several alcohol products are of international brands. The categorisation of industrial alcohol is made according to the alcohol concentration – 65 UP (20% alcohol), 40 UP (34%), 30 UP (40%), 25 UP (42.8%) and OP which is the measurement for beverages exceeding 42.8% alcohol content. Similarly beers produced in Nepal contain 5 to 7 per cent alcohol. Jawalakhel distillery, the prominent alcohol industry is currently producing 12 different brands of whiskey, rum, vodka and brandy out of which 3 are 25 UP, 3 are 30 UP, 5 are 40 UP and one is 65 UP products. According to VAT Department, 40 UP liquors were sold in maximum amount during the first half of the current fiscal year.

Table 4.1 displays the number, capacity of production and employment situation of the alcohol industries. According to data provided by VAT office, there are 56 distilleries, 5 breweries and five tobacco industries in Nepal.

Table 4.1 Types, Capacity, and Employment of Alcohol Related Industries in Nepal, 2000

Description	Amount
Distillery (Medium and Large Scale Industry)[2]	
No. of Industries	36
Capacity (Liters)	42,483,428
Employment (for only 23) in persons	1,458
Beer (Medium and Large Scale Industry)	
No. of Industries	8
Capacity (Liters)	50,000,000
Distillery (Small and Cottage Industry)[3]	
No. of Industries	24
Capacity (Rs.[4])	23,873,500
Employment in persons	569

Source: Ministry of Industry and Commerce, HMG, 2000.

The capacity of the alcohol production per year was 42,483,428 LP litres (1 LP litre is 57.08% spirit concentration) from medium and large-scale industries and 50,000,000.0 litres of beer from Breweries. The cottage and small-scale industries have reported their capacity of production in Rupees, that is, 23,873,500.0.

The production of alcohol has drastically grown in volume over the years. According to available data, the production alcohol has increased from 400 to 600 per cent in the last 10 years. Accordingly, the national revenue from alcohol has remained steady for the last seven years, exceeding 1 billion rupees mark (6 % of the total government revenues). Alcohol (liquors and beer) contributes more than 50 per cent to the total excise duty in Nepal. There is a 19 per

---

[2] Industry with a fixed asset from 30 to 10 million Rupees is called Medium Industry and with a fixed asset of more than 100 million Rupees is a Large Scale Industry.

[3] Industry with a fixed asset of up to 30 million Rupees is Small Scale Industry. Cottage Industries are those utilising specific skill or local raw materials and resources, and labour intensive related with national tradition, art and culture.

[4] Convertion rate was US$ 1=Rs. 74.5 at the time of study.

cent increment in alcohol production and 13 per cent increment in revenue collection during fiscal years 2055/56 and 2056/57 (Table 4.2).

Table 4.2 Revenue From Registered Alcohol Related Industries in Nepal

Type of Revenue	Fiscal Year – 2055/56	Fiscal Year - 2056/57[2]
VAT	230,089,740	281,150,838
Excise duty	-	1,717,170,000
Total	1,540,000,000[1]	1,998,320,838

[1] *Estimated by RECPHEC Nepal, 1998.*
[2] *Estimated based on half-yearly information, Department of VAT, Ministry of Finance, 2000.*

Yet, the actual amount of alcohol production may be far more than that recorded in VAT or Ministry of Industry. There is a strong tendency to evade tax by both the producers and tax collection officers.

4.2 Alcohol Economy at the Household Level

"Compared to the situation 20 or 30 years ago, the society is more open these days. The traditional demarcation between the drinkers and non-drinkers is narrowing down. There is no need anymore for people of higher caste to drink in secret, they can do so openly. There are many people belonging to Brahmin and Chhetri caste in my village who have started even to produce alcohol at their home, if not they ask others to brew for them and store cans and cans of liquor at home", says a social worker from Sunsari district.

The statement made by one of our key informants is illustrative of how the production and consumption of alcohol has spread across all caste/ethnic groups of Nepal in recent years. This is also evident from quantitative data where one third of the total households of Nepal produces alcohol (Table 4.3). Almost three-fifth households come from eastern development region. Similarly, around six in 10 traditional alcohol-user households produce alcohol at their home. The production of alcohol is also associated with the extent of poverty of the households. More than two-fifth of the total households with difficult livelihood around the year produce alcohol.

Table 4.3 Status of Alcohol Production by Households

Background characteristics	Alcohol production		
	Yes	No	N
Place of Residence			
Rural	40.5	59.5	1,437
Urban	21.4	78.6	844
Ecological zone			
Mountain/Hill	40.7	59.3	1,011
Kathmandu	33.6	66.4	146
Tarai	27.0	73.0	1,124
Traditional alcohol use status			
Traditional user	58.7	41.3	1,242
Traditional non-user	3.2	96.8	1,022
Unspecified	5.9	94.1	17
Livelihood			
Sufficient	31.4	68.6	1,849
Insufficient	42.1	57.9	432
Total	33.5	66.5	2,281

Note: Missing cases (52) were excluded.

People produce alcohol mostly on the occasion of feasts and festivals (67%). They also produce alcohol for commercial purpose (33%). Women are the main alcohol producers in the households (40.4% mothers, 44.1% wives, and 14% daughters and daughters-in-laws of the respondents). Households produce alcohol for three purposes: for family use, for sale and for both family use and sale. Majority of the households produce alcohol for sale, followed by family use.

Alcohol business is fully supportive to the household expenses for a notable proportion of the alcohol producers (15.4%). It is also partially supportive to the majority of the alcohol producers (Table 4.5).

Table 4.4 Description of Alcohol Production Among Alcohol Producers

Items of Responses	%	N
Season for alcohol production		
Feast/Festivals	67.0	511
Winter	2.4	18
Summer	1.7	13
Always	29.0	221
Alcohol producer in household		
Women (mother/wife/daughter)	98.5	752
Men (Father/husband/brother/son)	1.5	11
Purpose of alcohol production		
Family use only	13.0	99
Sales only	34.9	266
Both purposes	52.2	398
Total	100.0	763

Table 4.5 Support from Alcohol for Household Expenses

Support from alcohol for household	%	N
Sufficient	15.4	102
Partially sufficient	46.1	306
Insufficient	38.6	256
Total	100.0	664

Note: Don't know and non-response cases were excluded.

Why such a large proportion of alcohol producers are supported fully or partially in their household expenses from alcohol earning? It requires assessing the amount of alcohol production, consumption, selling, and earnings.

On the average, every household produces 30 manas, consumes 8 manas and sells 22 manas of alcohol per month and by which they earn Rs. 327.0 per month. This income is equivalent to the fourth-fifths of the total income of the 'untouchables' households in Nepal[5].

---

[5] The 'untouchables' per capita income was estimated to be RS. 4,940 (Nepal South Asia Study Centre, 1988:266).

For some hotel owners from remote parts of Nepal, alcohol selling has been a very profitable business. This is because they do not require a license for selling alcohol. Sometimes, police comes at their hotel, but takes some money and let them continue selling. Bishu, a hotel owner from a village of Dang, tells us:

> *"Alcohol is a profitable item in any shop or hotels, for other things you have to cook and serve but alcohol is sold straight. The peak season is during the big festivals where from rich to poor everyone wants to relax with drinks.*
>
> *I don't have a license to sell alcohol but I need to pay a sum of Rs. 1500.0 per year to the policemen. I had some policemen who came down form Bhalubang to demand explanation why I am selling seal packed liquors without license, I told them if no license is needed to drink, then why license is needed for selling?"*

In this study, a family in the Tarai produces 36 mana sells 26 mana, and consumes 10 mana of alcohol, whereas household in mountain/hill earns the highest income from alcohol, that is, Rs. 340.0 per month. There is no significant difference between rural and urban in terms of producing, selling, and consuming alcohol. Only the difference is observed in terms of earnings from alcohol, that is, a household in rural earns, on the average, Rs. 332.0 compared to Rs. 309.0 for urban areas.

The traditional non-users produce 42 mana, consume 9 mana, sells (33 manas) more alcohol and earns (Rs. 429.0) more than from traditional alcohol users do[6]. In some districts, such as Dang, Banke, Bardiya, Kailali and Kanchanpur where bonded labour system exists, often the traditional alcohol non-users produce alcohol at their home to serve it for their labour. Livelihood of the household is also associated with the production of alcohol in Nepal. The poorer the household, the more chances to produce alcohol at home for the purpose of selling it. In some locality for some ethnic groups it stands out to be the major source of income and is viable for the expenditure of children's schooling, clothing, and medicine as well. Despite the free education up to secondary level, households have to incur indirect cost of schooling of children such as admission fee, examination fee, books, and dress. One estimate indicated that on the average one household has to pay 50 per cent of the public sector

---

[6] Causation should be borne in mind that the sample of non-users is very small.

expenditure in Nepal (NASAC, 1998). A Police officer in Terahathum, says:

> *"Alcohol selling is the major source of income for people here. In the market area, 95 per cent people make a living out of it. The alcohol shops cater not only to the locals, but also to the travelers who come from all places. It is a transit place for travelers coming from Taplejung, Sankhuasava, Chainpur, etc. Women here are the alcohol producers and sellers and their men-folk depend upon their women for their livelihood. These women run household expenses by alcohol income, including children's school fees and clothes. Alcohol is important for family economy, perhaps that's why there is no protest here unlike many other districts. When there is no request from public, we can not start any alcohol control programme, there will be no support if we started such measures here. We have only made it a rule to close down hotels and restaurants after eight at night."*

It appears that alcohol production and selling is a major source of income for traditional alcohol user families, especially for women. For example, a household[7] with insufficient income around the year produces (42 against 30 mana), sells (30 against 23 mana), and consumes (12 against 7 mana). Per household earning per month is Rs. 400 for the poor households as against Rs. 306 of non-poor household (Table 4.6).

---

[7] A household with sufficient income around a year may be the non-poor household. However, this is the proxy indicator of poverty.

Table 4.6 Average Alcohol Production and Consumption, and Earnings During Last Month (in Mana)

Background Characteristics	Production	Selling	Income (in Rs.)	N	Consumption	N
Place of Residence						
Rural	33	25	332	509	8	322
Urban	34	25	309	154	8	75
Ecological zone						
Mountain/Hill	32	25	340	360	7	214
Kathmandu	19	18	233	45	1	13
Tarai	36	26	326	258	10	170
Traditional alcohol use status						
Traditional user	32	24	322	640	8	384
Traditional non-user	42	33	429	22	9	12
Unspecified	100	60	1,200	1	40	1
Economic sufficiency						
Sufficient	30	23	306	513	7	297
Insufficient	42	30	399	150	12	100
Total	33	25	327	663	8	397

Note: 1 mana = .05685 Litre (Ministry of Agriculture, 1996).

The economic contribution of alcohol in Nepal is substantial and it is also the major source of income in some of the poorest households. Still, the extent and pattern of alcohol use justifies the importance and spread of alcohol use in Nepal, which is the topic of the next chapter.

Chapter V

Extent and Pattern of Alcohol and Drug Use

This chapter is divided into two sections. The first section discusses the prevalence rates of alcohol, drugs and tobacco at the individual level[8]. The second section deals with the sociability of alcohol, drugs and tobacco in terms of their initiation, types, frequency and perceptions.

5.1 Extent and Patterns of Alcohol Use

The extent and patterns of alcohol use at the individual level are examined on the basis of experience of alcohol, experience within last 12 months, and experience within the last 30 days. Ever experience of alcohol is the ratio of ever alcohol users to the total respondents, which is estimated by asking question: "have you ever taken any alcohol beverage?" About 57 per cent of the total respondents ever experienced any type of alcohol in their lifetime (not shown in Table). This, however, is a crude measure because it will not include use that is really relevant for the current situation. Therefore, alcohol prevalence was examined asking question "Have you taken alcohol during the last 12 months? (Table 5.1). The overall alcohol use[9] is 41 per cent. The proportion of users, however, varies with age and gender of the respondents.

---

[8] The individual respondents were those who were at least 15 years old and able to respond to the questions.

[9] This is the ratio of current users (within the last 12 months) to the total respondents.

Table 5.1 Proportion of Respondents by Age and Gender Having Experienced Alcohol During Last 12 Months

Age	Male		Female		Total	
	%	N	%	N	%	N
6-17	18.8	96	19.6	51	19.0	147
18-24	42.7	206	18.4	147	32.6	353
25-34	56.5	306	27.2	265	42.9	571
35-44	55.7	345	32.7	168	48.1	513
45-54	55.0	262	30.4	115	47.5	377
55-64	45.5	176	35.3	51	43.2	227
65 and above	28.7	115	40.0	30	31.0	145
Total	48.3	1,506	27.7	827	41.0	2,333

For example, 48 per cent of the total males were currently using some type of alcohol while the comparable figure for females was 28 per cent. Two explanations of such high proportion of males currently taking alcohol could be: i) males can initiate drinking not only in their household but also outside their households while females are rarely exposed to alcohol outside of their home and ii) there may be few females from non-traditional alcohol user groups with exposure and access to alcohol.

Table 5.2 summarises the variation of current use of alcohol with the socio-economic characteristics of the respondents. There is a clear pattern of current use by place of residence. Respondents living in rural areas are more likely to use alcohol than that of urban areas. This is much pronounced in case of females. More than one-third of females in rural areas are currently using alcohol as against three in ten in urban areas. In rural Nepal, most traditional users of alcohol consume *Jand* (rice wine) as food.

This finding suggests that use of alcohol in Nepal may be determined by three factors: availability and accessibility of alcohol and the extent of people's mobility. When people migrate from one place to another, their tradition might gradually disappear and they may adopt new culture. This is true because mobility of Tarai population is not as much compared to the population in the hills/mountain. Similarly, access to and availability of alcohol is much higher in the capital city of Kathmandu than that of the rest in the country.

There is an inverse relationship between current use of alcohol and education of the respondents. Increasing education implies lower level of current use of alcohol. This variation is much wider for females. For example, more than one third of females with no education are currently drinking alcohol while the comparable figure for those females with SLC and above education is just 6 percentage points. This is instructive in the sense that increasing female's education may work as catalytic force for reducing alcohol use in Nepal.

There is also great variation of current use of alcohol by traditional users and traditional non-users. This gap is much pronounced for females. Almost 46 per cent of females belonging to traditional user are currently using any type of alcohol while the comparable figure for females belonging to non-traditional user category is only 3 per cent.

The indicator of alcohol use within the last 12 months covers a wide rage of duration and hence it does not typically show the proportion of regular alcohol users in the population. It can be precisely examined through the information of user within the last 30 days of the survey. Of the total respondents, 37.6 per cent are currently using alcohol within the last 30 days (Table 5.3). One-fifth of the respondents have taken alcohol for 1-5 days during the last 30 days of the survey. This proportion declines as the number of days increases in a month. Overall, 10 out of 100 respondents were daily alcohol users (20+ days). This variation is much pronounced while considering the gender dimension. More females over males tend to be non-users of alcohol. For example, almost half of the male respondents have currently taken any type of alcohol in the last 30 days, the comparable figure of females is just 21 per cent.

Table 5.2 Proportion of Respondents by Background Characteristics Having Experienced Alcohol During the Last 12 Months

Background Characteristics	Male %	Male N	Female %	Female N	Total %	Total N
Place of Residence						
Rural	49.8	902	33.9	561	43.7	1,463
Urban	46.2	604	14.7	266	36.6	870
Ecological regions						
Mountain/hills	48.5	618	38.9	409	44.7	1,027
Kathmandu	56.1	123	8.3	24	48.3	147
Tarai	46.9	765	17.3	394	36.8	1,159
Education						
No education	56.2	363	36.6	464	45.2	827
Primary	50.4	240	27.1	85	44.3	325
Secondary	41.6	358	15.2	138	34.3	496
SLC and above	46.2	331	6.4	94	37.4	425
Not stated	47.2	214	19.6	46	42.3	260
User Vs non-users						
Traditional users	65.8	787	45.8	474	58.3	1,261
Traditional non-users	28.2	703	3.4	351	19.9	1,054
Not specified	75.0	16			66.7	18
Total	48.3	1,506	27.7	827	41.0	2,333

**Table 5.3 Proportion of Respondents by Gender Having
Experienced Alcohol During the Last 30 Days**

Frequency of alcohol Use	Males		Females		Total	
	%	N	%	N	%	N
None	53.5	806	78.6	650	62.4	1,456
1-5 days	20.8	314	12.7	105	18.0	419
6-19 days	12.2	184	6.0	49	10.0	233
20+ days	13.4	202	2.8	23	9.6	225
Total	100.0	1,506	100.0	827	100.0	2,333

Six different types of alcohol were cited in the question to examine
what types the respondents had consumed these within the last 30
days of the survey. The alcohol consisted of *Jand* or *Chhang* (home
brews fermented from rice, millet, maize and wheat), home-made
Raksi (distilled liquor made of grains or unrefined sugar for
household use), local *Raksi* available at market (locally made for
commercial purpose), beer, distillery products (brandy, rum, vodka,
whisky) and foreign made liquors (wine, brandy, gin, whiskey etc.).

Among the different types of alcohol, *Jand/Chhang*, home made
Raksi and local *Raksi* available at market are the most common drinks
in Nepal. About 73 per cent of the total respondents have experienced
Jand/Chhang and 71 per cent experienced home made *Raksi* during
the last 30 days preceding the survey. Similarly, 55 per cent of the
total respondents experienced local *Raksi* available at market.
Industry produced alcohol such as beer, distillery products and
foreign products is also common drinks in Nepal. Almost 45 per cent
of the total respondents were currently using beer, one third of the
respondents were using distillery products, and a little less than one
fifth were using foreign products.

Except *Jand/Chhang*, the frequency of use within the last 30 days is
substantially lower for females than males by all types of alcohol. A
few females take beer, distillery products and foreign products.
Access to alcohol market is largely available for males. In Nepal,
females usually do not take alcohol in hotels and restaurants even if
she is from traditional user group. In the following section, we will
discuss why people take alcohol in Nepal.

Table 5.4 Proportion of Respondents by Gender Having Experienced Alcohol During the Last 30 Days by Type of Alcohol

Description	Male		Female		Total	
	%	N	%	N	%	N
Jand/Chhang	67.2	490	89.6	205	72.6	695
Home made *Raksi*	69.1	503	77.3	177	71.0	680
Local market *Raksi*	59.2	431	41.6	95	55.0	526
Beer	51.6	375	25.3	58	45.2	433
Distillery product	41.8	304	14.8	34	35.3	338
Foreign product	21.0	153	7.0	16	17.7	169

5.1.1 Reasons for Alcohol Use

Historically, in some communities of Nepal alcohol is an essential substance for their cultural, ritual and religious ceremonies. For example, most ethnic groups such as Tamang community[10], *Jand/Chhang* or home-made *Raksi* is required in death rituals. In some communities, *Jand/Chhang* is taken as substance food. This is also served for women during maternal period. Offering *Jand/Chhang* is a gesture of respect for guests. Our key informants reported the importance of alcohol in their cultural and ritual ceremenonies as

> *"We can not perform any rites without alcohol. I do not know when and how it started, but alcohol has a big significance in our religion and culture. It is compulsory during our various ceremonies such as kulayan (anscestoral worship), wedding, chewar (naming ceremony of newborn), and ghewa (death rituals). Alcohol is also important during social occasions, in fact, in our culture we honour somebody by serving alcohol. Of course, alcohol sometimes leads to arguments and fights, but the interesting thing is very often it is alcohol again which brings truce among the fighting parties. It is so easy, you just ask for forgiveness for creating disorder, just say that you lost your mind because of drinking and offer alcohol as 'Sagun', a friendly gesture for good omen", says a Tamang man from Nuwakot district.*

---

[10] Tamang is one of the oldest indigenous ethnic groups of Nepal. In the event of death ritual, *Ghewa*, there is a practice that requires all the close relatives to come in the deceased's house with *Raksi* . Such ritual often lasts for 12 days of the death of the family member. Excessive use of alcohol during such periods sometimes becomes matter of prestige for the household members of the deceased.

Some key informants also related the importance of alcohol in their community as a part of life. It is argued that alcohol production and consumption is the part of agrarian system in Nepal.

> *"Alcohol is significantly attached to the Limbu culture. Limbu are people residing in the hilly areas of Nepal, an agrarian economy. Before the unification of the country in the 18th century, the Limbu or Kirant people had the complete control over their resources - lands and woods. The production of grain was abundant, people cultivated different types of grains - rice, maize, millet. Millet is traditionally considered inferior grain and is largely used in alcohol brewing rather than as food. People celebrated life and seasons. Harvest was and is always a big happy event. Alcohol is a part of that celebration, it is a part of life. It was a part of relaxed, reliant, agricultural system", says a social activist from Terhathum district.*

Most key informants reported that it is not the alcohol produced at the household is a problem rather it is the commercialization of alcohol that has been destroying the fabric of our society. The major reasons for the commercialization of alcohol is reported to be political protection of alcohol production, consumption and distribution including lack of law enforcement.

> *" The share of the alcohol revenue is important in Nepalese economy, so the government does not want to control and stop the production and use of alcohol. If the government can not regulate the alcohol industries, it can not control the local or home production of alcohol as well. There are some laws and acts related to control and regulate the production and use of alcohol. But, they are completely ineffective. The related agencies are not able to implement the laws and acts", says a social worker from Kathmandu.*

At the individual level, people give various reasons for alcohol use (Table 5.5). 'Recreation' as a reason for taking alcohol appears to be the most important reported reason for taking alcohol in Nepal. Other reported reasons include 'part of food', 'to forget sorrow', 'medicine', 'problem solver', 'stimulator', 'status symbol', and 'social lubricant'. However, more females take alcohol as food substance and as painkiller and medicine.

Table 5.5 Reasons for Using Alcohol by Gender

Reasons	Male (n=1,005)	Female (n=322)	Total (n=1,327)
	%	%	%
Recreation	59.4	38.5	54.3
Part of food	9.8	20.5	12.4
To forget sorrow	9.6	13.7	10.6
Medicine	6.9	11.8	8.1
Problem solver	1.9	3.4	2.3
Stimulator (energiser)	2.1	2.8	2.3
Status symbol	1.4	1.6	1.4
Social lubricant	1.5	1.2	1.4
Others	7.6	6.5	7.3
Total	100.0	100.0	100.0

Heath (2000) argues that structured interview may not represent the actual feeling of people why they are taking alcohol. So he suggests that the reason for drinking be posed in an open-ended manner. The reasons that people give for drinking are many and varied such as taste, celebration, relaxation, mood alteration, hospitality, sociability, food and enhancement, pastime, religion, medicine and other. He interprets them as health, psychological, political, social, economic, religious and other reasons.

In our survey, we have employed both structured and unstructured interviews. Our findings very much tally with what Heath predicts as the types of response people would give. In the meantime with open-ended discussion with people we have some scope to analyse what are the context, influences and environments that determine people's motive for drinking.

Alcohol behaviour of people is much influenced by the familial and community environment of an individual where he or she is residing. In our study, some alcohol users stated that they were using alcohol in order to forget the sorrow in their family. The case of Madhu is a typical example how he first initiated taking alcohol and stopped for some years and again he started drinking.

"My parents and ancestors never even touched alcohol, along with other taboo foods such as chicken, pig and garlic. I learnt to drink in

1961 because I was in such a company. We are traditionally farmers,
but I got a job in a hydro-power company and was together with
people coming from different castes. For a 18 year old boy, it was a
time for discovery. I continued to drink till 1984, then I stopped and I
resumed drinking from 1992 when I lost my daughter. She killed
herself and the sorrow was too much", says a man aged 56 from a
traditional non-alcohol user group in Nuwakot.

5.2 Context of Alcohol Use

"I do not agree that drinking makes people popular and macho. I feel
that the underlying causes behind alcohol use is peer pressure, social
environment and unemployment and it is up to individuals to decide
whether they want to drink or not", says a man from traditional
alcohol user group, Pokhara.

For identifying individual contexts of alcohol use, three questions
were asked to the respondents: occasion, place, and time of alcohol
use. Table 5.6 shows the proportion of respondents who usually take
alcohol in a particular occasion by gender. Traditional and cultural
celebrations stand out the primary occasion for using alcohol.
Similarly, a large number of alcohol users take alcohol during the
social gatherings. Overall, three-fifth of the respondents usually take
alcohol in a particular type of occasion while the rest take alcohol at
no special occasion. The latter type of alcohol takers mostly come
from traditional non-user group where alcohol is not used for
religious or cultural purposes.

Table 5.6 Occasion for Using Alcohol by Gender

Occasions	Male (1,005)	Female (322)	Total (1,323)
	%	%	%
Traditional and cultural occasions	40.4	51.6	43.1
Social gatherings	18.0	10.2	16.1
No occasion required (any occasion)	41.6	38.2	40.8
Total	100.0	100.0	100.0

5.2.1 Environment of Alcohol Use in Family and Neighbourhood

Why such a large number of respondents are drinking at any time? It
is reported that insufficient supervision of children by parents,
conflicts in the family, parental use of alcohol at home, media and
peer influence, and easy availability are responsible factors prevailing

in the home as well as in the community. Insufficient supervision might arise from two reasons - ignorance of parents and absence of parent(s). Conflicts in the family might push children into using intoxicants. Parental use of alcohol at home induces children into initiation, because 'drinking is a learnt behaviour, which passes from elders to youngsters'. As a result, 'children learn drinking at young ages from their parents'. Media and peer influence expose children into the use of alcohol. Besides, there is a market forces that target children. For a long time, hard alcohol drink was made available in plastic *pouch*, attractive, easy to carry, low quality with low price, which was easily available everywhere. Only recently, a ban has been introduced in pouch alcohol following some deaths, including that of children from consumption of that liquor.

Such a conducive environment of alcohol use is the recent phenomenon among the groups where alcohol is disallowed traditionally. Some 20 or 30 years ago, drinking was entirely considered a taboo and those who took alcohol from this group were looked down upon, even excluded from the society. The story of Madhu tells us the transformation of our society into favourable environment for alcohol use.

> *"Coming from a Chetri family, I was aware about three things - one, alcohol is not allowed in our caste, secondly, it was a waste of money and thirdly, drinking meant loss of prestige. The social sanctions were so strict that it meant ever the loss of your caste. When I began drinking, I had to do it in secret. I had to hide my habit from all the elders in family and for about 10 years or so, I succeeded in that. But gradually my family got to know about my drinking, they were shocked. I lost my position in family, I was served food not on the main floor (where all the male members of family ate) but in the lower platform (where food was served to lesser people in the family hierarchy such as children)", says a Madhu, 56, from a traditional alcohol non-user family in Nuwakot.*

5.2.2. Socio-psychological Environment for Alcohol Use

Exposure to alcohol is largely determined by social environment in which respondents reside rather than individual choice alone. About 57.6 per cent of the respondents reported that they have had hotel, restaurant, bars or shops selling alcohol nearby their homes and at least 88 out of 100 respondents' reported their neighbors using alcohol

(Table 5.7). Two-fifth of the respondents said that there were 'many' alcohol users in their neighborhood while 26 per cent reported that there were 'some' and 29.6 per cent reported there were 'less' number of people using alcohol.

Table 5.7 Social Environment Influencing Exposure to Alcohol Use

Description	%	N
Are there restaurant/bar/shops selling alcohol in the community?		
Yes	57.6	1,314
No	42.4	967
Are there any alcohol users in the neighborhood?		
Yes	88.0	2,008
No	8.0	183
DK	3.9	90

Note: Missing cases (52) were excluded.

Favourable environment for alcohol and tobacco use is also due to the flooding of advertisements in print and other means of communication in Nepal. Advertisements change attitudes about drinking among young people. It is said that young people express more positive feelings of drinking and of their own livelihood to drink after viewing alcohol ads.

For the first time in Nepal, advertisement of alcohol/tobacco from electronic media was prohibited in February 1999. Since then electronic media provide health advertisements and anti-alcohol/tobacco advertisements during the news hours.

However, there is a flow of advertisement from print-media and other means of communications in Nepal. None of the weekly or daily papers is without the advertisement of alcohol or tobacco. For example, only on a month of January and February 2000, there were a total of 245 alcohol advertisements in 25 weeklies and daily newspapers. Similarly, in January- February, 1999, the Kantipur Daily- the most circulated daily newspaper in the private sector-provided a total of 297 advertisements for alcohol, 179 for beer, 238 for cigarette, and 356 for Khaini. The Gorkhapatra- the Government daily newspaper- during the same period provided a total of 33 alcohol advertisements and 10 tobacco advertisements. While a few welfare advertisements were available in these newspapers.

We also collected information on whether the media has had impact of using alcohol among children 10-17 years of age. Of the total children ever experienced alcohol, the highest percentage listen Radio Nepal daily (89.7%), followed by those who watch Nepal television (69.8%) and Nepali/Hindi movie in hall/video (63.8%), and by those who read Nepal Newspaper/magazine (48.3%). The percentage listening Radio FM is the least (11.2%) because it is only broadcast in Kathmandu Valley (Table 5.8). Besides, per centage of those reading English newspaper/magazine, watching English movie is also minimal. Among the media, only Radio Nepal and the Nepal TV are very common, whereas other media are less frequently used by alcohol users, that is once in a month. However, it is difficult to see the effect of media exposure on children's use of alcohol. Because, the respondents are mostly from rural areas where there is only radio available and television is partly available.

Table 5.8 Media Exposure Among Children Aged 10-17 Who Have Ever Experienced Alcohol

Types of Media	Daily	Weekend	Monthly	Total	Total N
Listen Radio Nepal	40.5	19.0	30.2	89.7	116
Listen Radio FM	4.3	2.6	4.3	11.2	116
Watch Nepal TV	29.3	11.2	29.3	69.8	116
Watch Satellite TV	12.9	9.5	14.7	37.1	116
Watch Nepali/Hindi Movie in Hall/Video	1.7	6.9	55.2	63.8	116
Watching English Movie in Hall/Video	-	1.7	17.2	18.9	116
Read Nepali Newspaper/Magazine	4.3	5.2	38.8	48.3	116
Read English Newspaper/Magazine	2.6	0.9	8.6	12.1	116
Read Film Magazine	0.9	3.4	30.2	34.5	116

Media may not be the contributing factor to expose people to the drug use because it is illegal affair. Thus, friend circle is the most important factor for initiating drugs. Of the total children interviewed 11.5 per cent reported that their friends use drugs (Table 5.9). Among users, more than two-thirds of the users have friends who use drugs. Of which, 52.6 per cent say some and 15.8 per cent say many of their friends use drugs. The proportion of those who have no idea about the use of drugs by their friends is also considerable. However, the users who have no friends using drugs are the least. Similarly, majority of the users (57.9%) reported that they have friends involved in selling drugs. It is interesting to note that more than two-third of users (68.4%) have used drugs due to their peer pressure. Information clearly demonstrates that peer role in using drug is significant.

Table 5.9 Proportion of Children Aged 10-17 Reporting Drug Use by Friends

Description	%	N
Drug use by friends		
Yes	11.5	49
No	88.5	377
Total	100.0	426
Friends using drug at least once a week		
Nobody uses drugs	5.3	1
Some	52.6	10
Many	15.8	3
DK	26.3	5
Friends selling drugs		
Yes	57.9	11
No	42.1	8
Peer pressure on drug use		
Yes	68.4	13
No	31.6	6
Total	100.0	19

5.2.3 Familial Environment for Alcohol Use

In addition to the community environment for alcohol and drug use, it is important to examine the existing situation of individuals at their family: whether family uses and/or produces alcohol in the family (Table 5.10). Majority of Nepalese households use alcohol in their family (54%) and mostly males.

Table 5.10 Familial Environment Influencing on Exposure to Alcohol use

Description	%	N
Is alcohol used in the family?		
Yes	53.7	1,225
No	46.3	1,056
Who uses alcohol in the family?		
Males only	31.0	695
Females only	1.0	24
Both	36.0	825
None	78.8	1805
Don't Know	3.5	79
Total	100.0	2,281

Note: 52 cases were missing and excluded from the analysis.

A question was asked when the use of alcohol becomes problem in the family. The overall response is mixed. Some view alcohol as a problem when it is uncontrolled (24.6%). Other regard alcohol as a problem when there is violence due to alcohol use. Others see the use of alcohol by their children in the family as a major problem. There were also respondents who consider alcohol use as vice and just having a taste of it also becomes a problem for them (Table 5.11). Such perceptions may be related with the differences in culture values. In Brahman community- the traditional non-user group, just tasting of alcohol may be taken as a problem while in traditional alcohol users, uncontrolled use may be taken as a problem.

Table 5.11 Perception of Alcohol Problem in the Family

Perception of problem of alcohol	%	N
Just tasting	6.8	154
Use by females	3.7	84
Use by children	12.9	295
Uncontrolled use	24.6	561
If drinking becomes violent	19.7	450
No user in family	32.3	737
Total	100.0	2,281

Note: Missing cases (52) were excluded.

5.3 Extent and Patterns of Drug and Tobacco Use

In this sub-section, we will discuss how many people use drugs and tobacco, how much do they use and what are their attitudes and knowledge about drugs.

The extent and patterns of five types of drugs were examined: Cannabis (ganja, bhang, charesh) (65/90), Heroin (smack, brown sugar) (2/90), Opium and opiates (codeine, methadone, morphine, pethidine, buprenorphine) (6/90), Tranquilisers (sedatives and hynotics) (7/90) and others (glue, boot polish, iodex, kerosene, petrol)[11] (10/90).

A question was asked whether the respondents have experienced any type of drugs and tobacco during the last 12 months preceding the survey (Table 5.12). Four out of 100 and 53 out of 100 reported that they had taken any type of drugs and tobacco respectively during the last 12 months of the survey, respectively. Both drugs and tobacco use widely varied by gender. Males taking drugs is more than five times higher than females do.

**Table 5.12 Proportion of Respondents Having Experienced Drugs
and Tobacco During the Last 12 Months by Gender**

Substance	Male	Female	Total	N
Drugs	5.4	1.1	3.9	2,333
Tobacco	67.7	27.4	52.8	2,333

Younger generation is much likely to have experienced drugs during the last 12 months as compared to the older generation because of the increasing exposure to the modern media such as cinema and foreign channels. They are more likely to imitate the role model of heroes who usually use drugs or tobacco or alcohol. Older generation are more exposed to the cannabis. Cannabis is mostly used in religious and cultural ceremonies in Tarai of Nepal. For example, during the festivals such as Shivaratri and Holi, people use bhang and ghotta, which are derivatives of cannabis.

How many of the respondents were regularly using drugs? This is

---

[11] These categories are consistent with the categories made by HMG/Nepal and UNDCP project, the Narcotic Drug Control Division, Ministry of Home, Nepal.

summarised in Table 5.13. More than 2 per cent of the total respondents have experienced drugs within the last 30 days of the survey. No females were drug users (20 days and above). Having identified the proportion of regular drug users, it is essential to understand the context and reasons for using drugs.

Table 5.13 Proportion of Respondents by Gender Having Experienced Drugs During the Last 30 Days

Categories	Male		Female		Total	
	N	%	N	%	N	%
No	1464	97.2	824	99.6	2288	98.1
Yes, on 1-5 days	21	1.4	1	0.1	22	0.9
Yes, on 6-19 days	10	0.7	2	0.2	12	0.5
Yes, on 20+ days	11	0.7	-	-	11	0.5
Total	1506	100.0	827	100.0	2333	100.0

5.4 Context and Reasons for Drugs Experience

Drug use is often associated with lack of proper guidance by parents and children's exposure to western culture. Some parents, especially father working aboard are often amiss during the growing age of their children. Such parents, though might make good money for the family are unable to supervise what the children are doing with the money. In households run by mothers where husbands are absent due to work or other reasons, it appears that some mothers are unable to control their grown-up youngsters. One of the key informants from Dharan states:

"In Dharan, the most used drug is tedigesic (buprenorphine injection), even young children like 13 year olds are using it. Besides, there is phencidyl (codeine containing cough syrup) and nitrazepam (sedative-hypnotic tablet). There are multiple causes behind the growing use of drugs here. Our survey has discovered that the major factors are social and cultural conflicts, which bring about several emotional problems to the families. Many youngsters here have their father employed in the British army, during the course, they have moved from remote villages in Nepal to Hong Kong and Brunei, and from there, they have settled in Dharan. Already they had to adjust to different cultures. Many teenagers grew up abroad in western culture after they returned they had to face difficulties. There is no job opportunity for them here, for example, and easily get into the unemployed peer groups. The fathers live abroad, even after pension they take job outside, the children are left with their mothers only."

Majority of young drug users were getting drugs from friends (N=44), followed by drugs sellers (N=21). Public places, own homes, and friend's places were the common places of drug use. A few drug users take drugs in lonely places, school and college grounds. Similarly, majority of drug users take drugs with their friends (Table 5.14).

Table 5.14 Context of Drug Use (in Number)

Description	Male	Female	Total
Place to get drugs			
Drugs sellers/peddlers	21	1	22
Drug users (Friends and others)	57	5	62
Drug stores	4	2	6
Place to use drugs			
Home	23	2	25
Public place	28	5	33
Friends' place	22	1	23
Lonely place	9	-	9
Company			
None	20	1	21
With friends and others	62	7	69
Total	82	8	90

5.5 Conclusions

Alcohol use has become common across different strata of population. The spread and widely practice of alcohol in Nepalese society should be understood in a broader framework of favourable environment in Nepalese society. The family, the community, the company and the media all contribute to the spread and growing demand of alcohol, not only among adults but also among children in Nepal. The problem is further accelerated due to growing use of drugs by children and youths residing in urban areas. This issue is raised in the next chapter.

Impact of Alcohol Use on Children's Lives

"Before dry zone, my shop was visited by people from all castes, age group and gender. People spent their last penny on alcohol even if they had nothing to eat at home. Now at least the children can eat", says an alcohol seller, Talamarang, Sinsdhupalchowk.

6.1 Alcohol and Drugs Use among Children

The prevalence of alcohol and drugs is examined based on the information on use during the last 12 months preceding the survey. The overall prevalence of alcohol use among children aged 10-17 is 17.4 per cent for current use. The prevalence among boys (21.8%) is about double that of girls (11.2%) indicating gender variation in using alcohol. It is natural that even among the traditional user families, boys are more exposed to the alcohol than girls. The use of drugs is also found to be substantial (3.1%), which is about four times higher among boys than girls. Similarly, the variation in use of tobacco among boys and girls is less compared to alcohol and drugs (Table 6.1).

Table 6.1 Proportion of Children Having Experienced Alcohol and Drugs During the Last 12 Months by Gender

Selected characteristics	(n=426)		
	Boys	Girls	Both Sex
Alcohol	21.8	11.2	17.4
*Drugs	4.4	1.1	3.1
Tobacco	14.5	9.6	12.7

*Note: *Classification of drugs is based on UNDCP classification and the detail is as follows:*

Cannabis: Ganja, bhang, charesh
Heroin: Smack, brown sugar
Opium &Opiates: Codeine, Methadone, Morphine, Pethidine, Buprenorphine, etc.
Tranquilisers (sedatives & hypnotic): Valium, Nitrazipam, Dizepam, Alprazolam, Ativan, Buscalm etc.
Others: Glue, boot polish, iodex, kerosene, petrol, etc.

Age of children seems to be vital for using alcohol, drugs, and tobacco. Higher age is apparently associated with the higher use of the substances. However, the variation between ages is more pronounced for tobacco that for drugs and alcohol (Table 6.2).

Table 6.2 Proportion of Children Having Experienced Alcohol and Drugs During the Last 12 Months by Age

Age group	Alcohol	Drugs	Tobacco	N
10-14	15.2	1.5	7.1	269
15-17	21.0	5.7	22.9	157

Besides age and gender, education appears to be clearly associated with alcohol use, that is, increasing education means decreasing prevalence of alcohol. The association between education and drugs and tobacco use is not clear (Table 6.3).

Table 6.3 Proportion of Children Having Experienced Alcohol and Drugs by Educational Attainment During the Last 12 Months

Education	Alcohol	Drugs	Tobacco	N
No education	31.9	5.6	20.3	69
Primary	16.8	2.0	6.7	149
Secondary	13.0	2.9	13.0	208

Having explained the current use of drugs and its main determinants, it is essential to examine the proportion of regular users in the sample population. The proportion of users within the last 30 days is low as compared to the proportion of users within the last 12 months for both alcohol and tobacco and that gender is marked for both substances. Only 9.2 per cent of the children reported that they used alcohol during last 30 days. This means the remaining 8.2 per cent, referring to 17.4 per cent prevalence, did not use alcohol during the last 30 days. The proportion of user during last 30 days is slightly higher among boys (10.1%) than among girls (7.9%). Among those who used alcohol during that period, the highest percentage reported that they used for 1 to 5 days and a few were regular users (20 days and more). The pattern is similar for both boys and girls. In case of tobacco, the proportion of children using tobacco is gradually decreasing as the number of days using tobacco is increasing. Children who used for more than or equal to 20 days are few (2.3%). The pattern of using tobacco among both boys and girls is similar to the use of alcohol (Table 6.4).

Table 6.4 Proportion of Children by Gender Having Experienced Alcohol and Tobacco During the Last 30 Days

	Number of Days			
	No	1-5 days	6-19 days	20+ days
Alcohol				
Boys (n=248)	89.9	7.3	2.0	0.8
Girls (n=178)	92.1	5.6	1.1	1.1
Total (n=426)	90.8	6.6	1.6	0.9
Tobacco				
Boys (n=248)	85.5	6.0	5.2	3.2
Girls (n=178)	91.6	5.1	2.2	1.1
Total (n=426)	88.0	5.6	4.0	2.3

In case of alcohol, the information on type of alcohol within the last 30 days was also obtained (Table 6.5). The result indicates that the proportion of children using alcohol decreases as the type shifts from more affordability to less affordability, from cheaper to expensive ones. For instance, the proportion decreases when the type is shifted from Raksi to beer and to distillery products. The frequency of alcohol use among girls is even less even though the gender pattern is similar to the total. However, *Jand/Chhang*[12] is the one they use regularly. This is naturally attributed to the wide use of *Jand/Chhang* in rural areas, especially among traditional alcohol users.

---

[12] All observations for girls are from traditional users.

**Table 6.5 Proportion of Alcohol Use by Children During the Last
30 Days**

Type of alcohol used	Boys (n=54)	Girls (n=20)	Total (n=74)
Jand/Chhang	88.9	100.0	91.9
Home made Raksi	50.0	65.0	54.1
Raksi at market	22.2	20.0	21.6
Beer	20.4	10.0	17.6
Distillery products	7.4	5.0	6.8

The preceding analysis shows the extent of alcohol and drug use
among children aged 10-17 years. It does not show which substance is
a gateway drug. This can be examined in the following section.

6.1. 2 Association Between Alcohol, Drugs and Tobacco

Positive association exists between ever use of alcohol and parents'
use (r=0.3581); between ever use of alcohol and ever use of tobacco
(r=0.2107); between current use of alcohol and current use of drugs
(r=0.4880); between current use of alcohol and current use of tobacco
(r=0.3569); and between ever use of drugs and ever use of tobacco
(r=0.4304). Almost all the associations are moderate and statistically
significant at 0.05 level (Table 6.6).

Table 6.6 Correlation Among Alcohol, Drug and Tobacco Use

Variables	Alcohol use		Parent	Drugs use		Tobacco use	
	Ever use	Current	Parent	Ever	Current	Ever	Current
Children's ever use of alcohol	1.000						
Children's current use of alcohol	-	1.000					
Parent's use of alcohol	**0.358	-0.059	1.000				
Children's ever use of drugs	0.072	0.134	-**0.144	1.000			
Children's current use of drugs	-0.109	*0.488	-0.108	-	1.000		
Children's ever use of tobacco	**0.211	-0.036	-0.085	-**0.430	0.205	1.000	
Children's current use of tobacco	-0.020	*0.357	-0.110	0.118	-0.161	-0.050	1.000

*Note: * Significant at 0.01 level (2 tails) and ** Significant at 0.05 level (2 tails).*

It appears that the use of alcohol, drugs, and tobacco is positively associated each other. This indicates alcohol use by children can be attributed to parents' use of alcohol and to their use of drugs as well as tobacco. Use of drugs may be attributed to the use of alcohol as well as tobacco. Similarly, the use of tobacco may be attributed to use the of both alcohol and drugs.

6.1.3 How Children Initiate Alcohol and Drug Use?

Early childhood is affected by the use of any type of substance. Children are most prone to have in early exposure to alcohol in the rural areas. Information clearly shows that the median age of initiation is lower for alcohol (10 years) compared to drugs (13 years) and tobacco (13 years). Gender variation in use of substances is found only in drugs that girls started using one year later (14 years) compared to boys (Table 6.7).

Table 6.7 Median Age (in Years) of Initiation of Alcohol and Drugs by Gender

Types of substance	Boys	Girls	Both sexes
Alcohol (n=109)	10	10	10
Drugs (n=19)	13	14	13
Tobacco (n=54)	13	12	13

The reason for relatively lower median age for initiation of alcohol can be justified by the report of key informants. Among traditional user communities, cultural and religious ceremonies and social gatherings are considered as a gateway of initiating alcohol use for both children and adults. For these communities, alcohol is the major offering to gods and ancestors and is the main item to welcome and pay respect to guests and relatives.

Traditional and cultural occasions appear to be the most important occasion of initiating alcohol. Sixty out of 100 children reported that they initiated alcohol on such occasions, while the corresponding figures for boys is 67 per cent and for girls it is 46 per cent. The next majority reported that there were no special occasions (38%) when they had their first drink. Traditional and cultural occasions are found to be most responsible for boys and there is no special occasion (53.7%) for girls to initiate alcohol use (Table 6.8). This may indicate that there is somehow gender role in sociability of alcohol that boys gain more exposure than girls to the traditional and cultural functions to use alcohol.

Table 6.8 Proportion of Children Initiating Alcohol in Different Occasions by Gender

Description	Boys (n=75)	Girls (n=41)	Total (n=116)
Occasions			
Traditional/cultural	66.7	46.3	59.5
Social gatherings	4.0		2.6
No special occasion	29.3	53.7	37.9
Company			
None	8.0	22.0	12.9
Parents	44.0	43.9	44.0
Relatives/Friends	48.0	34.1	43.1
Total	100.0	100.0	100.0

Initiation to alcohol is entirely related with our traditional and cultural rituals, while the initiation of drugs is a complex process. Different drug users initiate using drugs in different context. Sometimes it is related with a fragile family environment, sometimes it is related with school environment and sometimes with the company. One of our key informants, Tej Bahadur from Dharan tells the story of his 19-year old son's taking drugs as:

> "I think there were two reasons for him to get into this habit – first, his school did not have any control mechanism, and secondly his mother spoiled him too much. When he was growing up, I was busy in my work, did not stay home for long, and the mother could not control the boy. Now the mother is most affected, if somebody says something about the youngest son, she begins to cry. It is not that I did not try to give him opportunity to get out of this habit. His brother working in Hong Kong sent money so we could send the boy to Malaysia for work. We spent Rs. 70,000, but his mother began to cry so we called him back spending another Rs. 35,000. Then I sent him again to Delhi and Bombay, in hopes that he will find something useful to do and change himself, But each time, he would be back once the money in his pocket is finished. My biggest problem is this boy."

Availability of drugs has also made tremendous increase of drug users among youth and children in urban areas of Nepal. Many drugs are reported to be available in Jogamani, the border town of India. One of our key informants reported that many youths make money buying drugs cheaply from Jogamani and selling them in Dharan at a higher price. If they bring 50 bottles of injection, they will make a fair amount to finance their drug habit.

Having examined the prevalence of alcohol and drugs among children and factors contributing to initiate these substances, it is essential to see the impact of alcohol use by adults on children's life.

6.2 Impact on Children's Life: Adult Perceptions

What is the impact of using alcohol in the family on children's life? This is summarised in Table 6.9. The major impact reported includes violence and physical abuse (33.4%), neglect and mental abuse (28.5%), deprived from education (20.2%) and children started to use alcohol (11.1%), malnutrition and run away from home. Broadly, the impact of alcohol use on children's life can be categorised into social impact and economic impact on children's life.

Table 6.9 Impact of Alcohol Use by Adult Members on Children's Life

Types of Problem	%
Violence and physical abuse	33.4
Neglect and mental abuse	28.5
Deprived from education	20.2
Children starting to use	11.1
Shortage of food/malnutrition	3.4
Run away from home	3.0
Others	0.4
N	470

Social impact perceived by the key informants are 'abuse and violence against women and children', 'looked as status symbol', 'cross caste barrier', 'lack of supervision to the children' and 'health related'. Sometimes alcohol is taken as a status symbol in the society as indicated by a key informant in our sample. Ram Bahadur, a teacher says:

"If a person who can afford the use of alcohol in an expensive hotel and restaurants in our community, he is symbolized as a high-class

elite or person. This, in turn, encourages the use of alcohol. Another thing is that the use of alcohol has crossed the caste barrier in the society.

Concerned about how Hindu hierarchical caste system losing its ground, he says "the differences between the various caste hierarchies prevailed in the Hindu society have been gradually decimating due to the use of alcohol."

It appears that women are much concerned about men's drinking behaviour. One of our key informants, Uma, from a village of Dang was terribly frustrated with her husband's drinking habit.

"I belong to non-drinking caste, but my husband, who is a school teacher, drinks excessively. When I got married, they told me my husband had no bad habit of drinking. After marriage I discovered that he drank a lot and his family members did not control him. I advised him many times to stop drinking but he does not listen to me. I have small children, they become scared when they see their father coming home drunk. The children are ashamed when people call them alcoholic's children. My little daughter smells her father's mouth to see if he has been drinking. My son feels concerned that if his father is spending all the money on alcohol then who will pay for his school."

Excessive use of alcohol often results in loss of wealth, which causes people to get into debt and to poverty. Then, people can not afford children's schooling, leading to likelihood of children to drop out from school. This situation is associated with high magnitude of child labour scenario, especially worst forms, where children can be economically exploited, psychologically abused/neglected, physically tortured and socially manipulated for work not suiting their age and capacity. This is also evident from Uma's husband drinking behaviour.

"Previously we had enough land, a lot has been sold by now. We have only 8 kattha, it is not enough to see us through. My husband is already running high debts, he does not even bring whole salary from school. Sometimes he does not return home for 4-5 days, he goes into drunken spree with his friends. Nobody in the village will give us any money now during emergency as my husband has borrowed from all of them."

Excessive use of alcohol is also linked to the economic exploitation in some communities of Nepal. One of our key informant from Nuwakot reported that most of the traditional alcohol user groups have lost their land due to the excessive use of alcohol and the land has been mortgaged by the upper caste people, traditionally alcohol-non user groups.

> *"There is an interesting situation regarding attitude towards alcohol among Brahmin/Chetri and Tamang people. Before, alcohol was often a means to take over other people's lands and wealth. For example, Brahmin/Chetri did not use alcohol themselves, but took advantage of Tamangs who did. The poor Tamangs had to mortgage their lands and borrow from the moneylenders in order to brew alcohol that was required in large quantity during their many rituals and celebrations. Alcohol ruined people this way, it was a means of exercising power by the higher caste to the lower", says a VDC representative from Nuwakot district.*

Some of our female key informants reported that their husband's excessive use of alcohol has made them very sad and they tried to kill themselves. It has been reported that the excessive use of alcohol was much pronounced among non-traditional user males than that of their counterparts. In our sample, Rita from Morang was such a woman who was complaining her husband's drinking behaviour:

> *"I am very tensed because of this situation, when he lies in the street completely drunk, I am very worried. Sometimes I want to kill myself, but there are my children. I feel very sad that coming from non-drinking culture my husband has gone overboard. The problem is less among Dhimals who have been drinking traditionally."*

6.2.1 Children's Perception

> *"My youngest son does nothing but use drugs. He uses every kind of drug that is available, including injection. He drinks alcohol also. He is so addicted that he will sell anything to get money to buy these things. Last time, he sold a bag full of nuts that were drying in the roof. Whenever he is send for errand, he disappears with the money. He takes loans in the market, giving my name and I have to pay it back. He has been like that since his high school days. He started using drugs when he was in class seven or eight", says a parent from Dharan about his 19 year old son.*

This section examines the impact of parent's as well as children's use of alcohol on children's lives. The analysis is based on the responses from interview of children aged 10-17 years. As mentioned above, impact of parent's excessive use of alcohol on children's lives is considerable. First, impact on home environment of alcohol use is examined based on the information on psychological as well as physical impact of alcohol use at home. This may affect children's lives in one way or another. Perception about impact of parents' drinking on family as a whole is presented in Table 6.10. Of the total children, a considerable proportion of children (35.9%) feel that there is impact of parents drinking on family. For those who reported that they have experienced impact of parents drinking on family, the another question on types of impact was asked. The children that they had experienced domestic violence (40%) in the family and 27.8 per cent reported that their family has lost wealth and was indebted due to use of alcohol. The equal percentage of children reported that they lost social prestige and their relationship with neighbour was soured. The pattern is similar to both traditional and non-traditional users.

Key informant interviews also support this finding. Most of the informants report that the use of alcohol in the family affects children's educational as well as mental development. It causes loss of wealth and people to get into debt, which in turn results in inability to pay for children's education. Many key informants make direct connection between drop-out of children from schools and expense of parental drinking. In addition, children face mental stress when parents drink excessively.

Table 6.10 Impact of Parent's Drinking on Home Environment

Description	Traditional users		Traditional non-users		Total	
	N	%	N	%	N	%
Impact of parents drinking on family						
Yes	73	36.3	17	34.0	90	35.9
No	128	63.7	33	66.0	161	64.1
Total	201	100.0	50	100.0	251	100.0
Types of impact on family due to parents drinking						
Domestic violence	30	41.1	6	35.3	36	40.0
Loss of social prestige	7	9.6	6	35.3	13	14.4
Bad relation with neighbour	13	17.8	-	-	13	14.4
Loss of wealth/debt	20	27.4	5	29.4	25	27.8
Illness/death	1	1.4	-	-	1	1.1
Others	2	2.7	-	-	2	2.2
Total	73	100.0	17	100.0	90	100.0

Types of impact as perceived by children due to their parent's use of alcohol is examined (Table 6.11). Of the total children interviewed, a considerable proportion of children (29.4%) reported that impact of parent's use of alcohol on children life exists. Among those who perceived impact, the overwhelming majority reported the type of impact is mental abuse like neglect and scolding (81.1%). Other types of impact like physical abuse, malnutrition/ starvation, encouragement to use alcohol and no schooling are equally perceived. The children from traditional user groups follow the similar pattern, whereas children from traditional non-user group perceived only two types of impact, that is, scolding (93%) and starting using alcohol (7.1%) by themselves.

Table 6.11 Impact of Parents' Drinking on Children's Life

Whether any impact on respondents	Traditional users		Traditional non-users		Total	
	N	%	N	%	N	%
Yes	60	29.9	14	27.5	74	29.4
No	141	70.1	37	72.5	178	70.6
Total	241	100.0	185	100.0	426	100.0
Types of impact						
Mental abuse (neglect, scolding)	47	78.3	13	92.9	60	81.1
Physical abuse (beating, torture)	4	6.7	-	-	4	5.4
Malnutrition/starvation	3	5.0	-	-	3	4.1
Encouraged to drink	3	5.0	1	7.1	4	5.4
Lack of schooling/ drop-out	3	5.0	-	-	3	4.1
Total	60	100.0	14	100.0	74	100.0

The impact of drug use and/or trafficking is much immense than that of alcohol on children's lives. Some of our key informants reported that their children were jailed for several months for abusing and/or peddling of drug use. One of our key informant's son from Dharan was jailed for six months after he was arrested for selling phencidyl and drug injections. It is a complex process to intervene young people using alcohol and drugs and it is equally challenging how to prevent people from harmful use of alcohol and drugs. This can be addressed by the mobilisation of multiple stakeholders ranging from individual, family, community to national legislation and international communities. This will be discussed in the next chapter.

Chapter VII

Counter-forces for the Prevention of Alcohol, Drugs, and Tobacco Use

This chapter deals with the counter-forces for the prevention of alcohol and drug use in Nepal. For this purpose, first, the existing laws and acts regarding regulation of alcohol and drugs are reviewed. Second, social and community level actions and movements against drugs and alcohol are presented. Finally, we will discuss the major counter-forces for the prevention of substance abuse.

7.1 Existing Laws and Regulations Regarding Alcohol and Drugs

a. Alcohol Act, 2031 B.S.[13]

This Act made basically four provisions for the control of liquor sale:

- License issue and renewal
- Right of raid (in the condition of illicit alcohol production) to VAT officers
- Punishment for defaulters (tax evasion, invalid license, unlawful activities) and rewards for information on illicit alcohol production.

Articles 3, 4 and 5 of the Act state the provision of production, sale and export/import of alcohol. Article 3 controls the production of alcohol without license or the conditions set by the license. According to article 4, no one is allowed to sell or distribute alcohol without license or the conditions set by the license to any bar or restaurant or

---

[13] B.S. refers to the Nepali Calender known as Bikram Sambat. The new year starts from about mid of the April. 2001AD is 2058 B.S.

shop. Article five prohibits of importing or exporting of alcohol without the license or the conditions set by the license.

Similarly, section 17 of the Act states that the Act will not hinder any one who has received a license or contract to produce alcohol from distilleries according to the current Nepal Law. This act does not, however, provide adequate provision for the restriction of sale except prohibition to those who are under 18 years of age. It provides little provision of the restriction of alcohol advertising in the media. Further, it fails to recognise alcohol use as problem rather than is taxable asset.

b. Hotel Regulations and the Sale and Distribution of Alcohol Act, 2023 B.S.

The main provisions of the Act regarding sale and distribution of alcohol are as follows:

- Control of the sale and serving of alcohol by hotels or shops (According to Section 3, hotels or shops which have provision to serve alcohol are allowed to sell alcohol from 12 noon to midnight on week days and from 12 to 1 AM on Fridays.
- Duty of the hotel owner (not serving excessive alcohol to the customer and alcohol should be served inside the hotel)
- Prohibition of selling and servicing alcohol to children and persons intoxicated with alcohol (Section 7 protects children under 16 years)
- Possibility of prohibition the sale and use of alcohol in a fixed area (Govt. can prohibit any hotel or restaurant selling and distributing of alcohol with a notice).

b. National Broadcasting Act, 2049 B.S.

This act discourages the advertisements for alcohol substances from print-media. However this act does not prohibit the advertising of alcohol substances. There is a tax of Rs. 105 for advertising alcohol.

c. Vehicle and Transport Regulation Act 2049 B.S.

The main objective of this act is to prohibit the use of alcohol or any other intoxicating substance by drivers while driving a vehicle.

Violation of this rule would cause fine of Rs. 25 for the first time, Rs. 50-60 for the second time and Rs. 100-200 for the third or more time.

The provision of fine envisaged by the Act is too low in which the rule offender would easily escape by giving money to the police or other authorities.

d. Local Administration Act, 2028 B.S.

Article nine of the Act allows the CDO to arrest any person behaving in an unsociable manner due to alcohol use. CDO can fine a maximum of Rs. 100 each time the person repeats the same mistake.

Many dry-zones in Nepal are under this Act. Since the purpose of the act is only to control the use of alcohol in case of violation or social unrest, the sustainability of dry-zone is questionable.

e. Alcohol Rules, 2033 B.S.

This rule is formulated under the Alcohol Act 2031. It states that no one is allowed to sell alcohol in any form within the public places such as compound of a temple, educational institution, school and college or within the 200 yards of those institutions. If alcohol use is required by religious purposes, permission is needed from the CDO.

f. Alcohol (First Amendment) Act, 2056 B.S.

This act came in the context where a massive amount of alcohol is produced and distributed using plastic known as pouch. In article 3, it prevents production and distribution of alcohol in two conditions: producing or selling alcohol in plastic packet known as pouch and selling it to children aged below 6 years.

These legal measures appear to have addressed alcohol mainly in economic term rather than in social or medical term. Despite introduction of multiple acts, the challenge lies in their effective implementation and no effective network system has been set up to operate the law. Generally, Ministry of Home is responsible to implement alcohol control laws in collaboration with Ministry of Industry, Ministry of Communication and Ministry of Health. But there is no formal institution to co-ordinate the activities of such Ministries regarding the control and/or prevent of alcohol use.

The laws do not recognize alcohol as matter of any social dimensions other than economic concern. All legal provisions on alcohol concentrate on the business role such as production, distribution and taxes. The alcohol policies are fairly conducive to alcohol industry. It implies scant restriction on advertisements. Only recently (1999) the ban of alcohol advertisement on electronic media has been introduced, and government has started to impose health tax on alcohol. According to information provided by VAT office, the taxation on alcohol products comprises of four components - excise duty (Rs. 32 per litre of beer and Rs. 235, 125 and 42 respectively for a LP litre of 25 UP, 30 UP and 40 UP alcohol respectively), health tax (Rs. 10 per LP litre), alcohol control tax (10 per cent of health tax) beside VAT charges. The health and alcohol control tax is utilised in counter-advertisements in radio and television making people aware of health and social risk arising from alcohol and tobacco use. Such efforts are new and their impact is still to be seen in making a difference at alcohol/tobacco control.

Most laws are violated in every aspects of life. License provisions and hotel or restaurant's regulations are weakening due to lack of supervision and corruption, and print media are being attracted by good money from the alcohol producers.

Alcohol rule 2033 V.S. can not be easily operationalised. There is a business holders' pressure vis-à-vis political leaders not to announce the dry-zone in the country. Political commitment is urgently needed to implement such laws even in the limited basis. The burning example is from Doti district. Doti district was declared a dry zone in 1997 but could not be sustained more than one-year. The primary reason for this was the misuse of the fine collected from those who violated the dry-zone norms. People complain that money was illegally used by CDO, DSP and District Chairman.

Another example is from Nuwakot district, a recently introduced dry-zone area at the time of the survey. Some political leaders are against the dry-zone and have exerted constant pressure to the local administration to revoke dry-zone. Some people from the area claim that dry-zone is a ploy to discourage local production of affordable alcoholic beverages and monopolize the market for more expensive industrial and foreign products. Some people from alcohol user communities also feel it as an onslaught to their indigenous culture.

7.1.1 National Drug Control Policy of HMG/Nepal

Nepal has given a serious attention to drug control since the mid-seventies. After that, several initiatives have been taken (Appendix 4). At present, the aim of the drug control policy is to "create, using socio-culturally acceptable strategy, a national climate where the non-medical use of drugs is virtually non-existent, leading to enhanced quality of life, higher rates of national development, and more efficient release and harness of human potential (Ministry of Home Affairs, 1996:9)." In order to achieve such aims, the following broad goals and programme have been determined.

Goals	Programmes
Law enforcement	to prevent cultivation, production, manufacture, trafficking, pushing of any type of narcotics
	to bring about a progressive reduction of drug-related crime, accidents and imprisonment
Harm reduction	to control/regularise the produce, import and sale of illicit substances
	to reduce personal, family and social harm
Demand reduction	to reduce the demand of drugs by raising the awareness among youths
Social support	to provide support for drug induced disabilities
Treatment and rehabilitation	to provide effective accessible, affordable and culturally acceptable treatment/rehabilitation facilities
	to provide social reintegration and economic empowerment
Legislative support	to support or ensure law enforcement
International obligations	to co-operate with international efforts in controlling drugs
Implementing agencies and system	to establish and strengthen institutions and projects

The Government has committed to implement these policies within the Ninth Five-year Development Plan (1997-2002) and some of the policies are expected to be continued. The Government's aim in combating drugs use appears to be ambitious. There is no effective co-ordination among the NGOs, INGOs and line ministries resulting in the duplication of research and action programme. Lack of trained human resources is another challenge.

Local Governments such as Municipalities and Village Development Committees are becoming aware of drug problems. They are also supporting activities of NGOs and CBOs.

Response of Local Government on Alcohol and Drug Problem

"Dharan is known as the place for retired army men. The residents here mostly belong to Mongol caste, so there is a high consumption of alcohol here. Along with alcohol, drug is a big problem here. Drug addiction here has risen from family concern to serious social concern. Different local organisations such as Yakthum Chumlung, Punerjeevan Kendra and mother groups are running public awareness programmes and anti-drug campaigns."

7.1.2 Existing Laws and Regulations Related to Children

There are a number of laws and acts for regulation and control of alcohol and drugs in Nepal. Most of them do not address adequately restriction of sale except prohibition to those who are under 18 years of age. There are only a few laws and acts addressing children regarding alcohol and drug use.

Child Act 1992, Provision 16 prohibits the use of children in selling alcohol, drugs and other illegal substances. Hotel Regulations and the Sale and Distribution of Alcohol Act, 2023 V.S., Section 7 has a provision on prohibition of selling and servicing alcohol to children under 16 years and persons intoxicated with alcohol.

Recently, a Bill (June 2000) banning the production and sale of the *Pouch* liquor (low quality with low price) and banning the sale of alcohol to minors (under 16) was tabled in the parliament. The Bill, which was the 2000 ammendment of the Alcohol Act 2031 V.S., is expected to be exercised soon.

7.2 Household and Community Level Counter-forces of Alcohol Use

Utilising the both structured and unstructured instruments, information on household and community level counter-forces in relation to alcohol use was obtained. Accordingly, this section deals with the counter-forces to the alcohol production, selling and consumption perceived by the respondents at two different levels: household and community levels. In the former, the perception of the survey respondents (adult member of the household) is analysed. In the latter, analysis is carried out on the basis of the key informants' interviews.

7.2.1 Household Level Counter-forces

In Nepalese context, family is the basic unit of decision making in every aspect of life. In the family, it is the head of the household, mostly man, who pulls the resources, allocates it among its members and decides who should do what. Any attempt to control or reduce alcohol consumption should focus on the family, especially head of the household, and make them aware of the disadvantages of excessive use of alcohol. Therefore, the responses suggested by the adult members to control or reduce alcohol consumption at the household can have greater policy implications.

A range of responses is listed in Table 7.1. They include regulation or control of production and selling, regulation and control of alcohol use, and raising awareness at the family level. Majority of respondents were in favour of controlling production and selling of alcohol. Similarly, a substantial number of respondents stressed the need to focus on family, especially head of the household.

Table 7.1 Efforts Needed to Reduce/Control Alcohol Use at Home (n=2323)

Efforts suggested by respondents	%
Controlling production and selling	43.8
Regulation and prohibition of alcohol use	21.0
Awareness in the family	19.8
Don't know	3.5
No responses	11.8

Such phenomenon could not have been found before 1990s where there was no legal provision to organise a civil society in Nepal. It is after the Democracy in 1990 that people became aware of social problems through their social institutions. In this context, the widening desire of regulating and prohibiting of alcohol production, consumption and selling can be partially the result of the impact of the work of different NGOs, CBOs and ethnic group organisations.

Some ethnic groups' organisation are focusing on the reduction of excessive use of alcohol at both household and community level. Their slogan "do not consume alcohol all the time, by everybody, in every amount" stresses the need to make distinction on the time, amount and individual regards to drinking. One of the organisations is Yakthum Chumlung, a Limbu indigenous group dedicated to the promotion and preservation of Limbu language and culture, and protection and promotion of human rights including indigenous people's right. One of its major activities is to provide treatment and rehabilitation facilities for drug abusers from residential treatment centre.

Such organisations are also able to define problem of alcohol in their culture. In some culture, mere experimenting with alcohol becomes a vice while in most ethnic groups such as among Limbus, it appears to be a problem when people become violent with alcohol use. There has been a lot of changes in the alcohol production at the household level. Expansion of education among the lower social strata of people is widening and local production is almost replaced by distillery product and commercialisation of alcohol.

Most ethnic groups perceive that anti-alcohol movement directed to the prohibition of alcohol started from the western hill regions of Nepal may not be replicated in most ethnic dominant areas as alcohol becomes their culture and life. One of the differences between western hill regions and other parts of Nepal is that the former has a majority of Chhetri and Brahman- the non-traditional alcohol users while the rest of the country has mixed ethnic groups and caste. In the former, women are non-users who started anti-alcohol movement while in the latter women themselves are alcohol producers and users.

Perception of Kirat Yakthum Chumlung on Alcohol

In socially accepted drinking culture, where does alcohol begin to become a problem?

"Different people react to alcohol in different ways. In our culture, people impose their own control system, shouting, physical violence and many kinds of misbehaviour are intolerated. If people get drunk and quietly go to their own way, it is not considered a problem. It is largely up to the individual, if you can say no to helping of food when you had enough, you can say know to alcohol as well while you are served. Of course in the mixed society, the whole meaning of drinking has different connotation, but in Limbu society, people who drink have to cater to certain social rules. They can not just go berserk. People who drink excessively are not looked down well by the community, hard drinking men have difficulties finding a wife. Everything has to be done under the social control in order to be accepted well by the community."

How do you look at the anti-alcohol movements that demand for dry zones?

"Dry zone concepts are counter-productive, the movement started in from the western Nepal where women suffered due to males drinking. The same model can not be fitted in the east because here women themselves are consumers. People produce and drink at home, its done in a way which is not problematic for anyone. Dry zone movement will not succeed in our parts."

Another question was asked who could be the effective agent to control or reduce the alcohol consumption at the household level. Most respondents regard men could be the effective agents, followed by women and elderly (Table 7.2). In patriarchal society like Nepal, the role of men in controlling alcohol consumption still remains imperative. However, women started most of the anti-alcohol movements in Nepal and their role in controlling alcohol should not be minimized. It is the women who first face the problem of alcohol at the household. They are abused, neglected and abandoned due to the excessive use of alcohol by their counterparts. In this context, women could be the main actors in combating alcohol problem.

7.2.2 Community Level Counter-forces

National level anti-alcohol movement has not yet started in Nepal. There is news that local level anti-alcohol movements have been increasing in Nepal. Such movements are largely led by women's groups, local government, NGOs and Community Based Organisation, some political parties and police. This process has started after the restoration of democracy in 1990.

Table 7.2 Main Actors to Reduce/Control Alcohol Use at Home as Perceived by the Respondents

Agents	N	%
Men	783	33.6
Women	701	30.0
Elderly	287	12.3
Other relatives	143	6.1
Son/daughters	62	2.7
No responses	357	15.3
Total	2,333	100.0

A massive anti-alcohol movement was initiated by women in west Nepal in early 1990s. By now, 40 districts of the country were declared 'dry-zone' by the local governments. Starting from Accham district, the movement spread to western Nepal and to the central and eastern parts of the country.

This movement came under the Local Administration Law, 1968 as there is no specific law against alcohol and no specific government body to address this issue. Under the complaints from local people, CDO or DDC act and through the approval of these local government bodies, the central government can issue the declaration of 'dry-zone'. The 'dry-zone' implies an area where alcohol is prohibited for both sale and production. The provision depends upon the local community but normally prohibits the public drinking and selling of alcohol. One of our key informants, Laxmi reported us the effect of anti-alcohol movement in her village- a village of Sindhupalnchow as:

> *"There has been a control in public alcohol consumption in this area since last two three years when there was an effort from VDC level for alcohol control. The chairman started anti-alcohol campaign, local alcohol was destroyed. Locally elected members, men and women together had organized protest rallies, campaigns and raids. So you can not see open shops selling alcohol in this area. We do not see any more people carrying gallons of alcohol to sell. But that has not cut down on people's consumption in privacy, we have not completely succeeded in controlling alcohol. We have heard that they sell alcohol only at night. Those who want find a way to get alcohol and continue to drink."*

The effectiveness and sustainability of anti-alcohol movement is questionable. In some districts such as in Doti such movement could not survive more than one year whereas in some districts such as

Accham this movement has continued for eight years. One of the main reasons of failure of anti-alcohol movement is politics of securing votes on the part of follow-up committee, weakness of main committee and administration and the aspiration of businessmen and general people to earn millions of Rupees overnight (The Kathmandu Post, September 6, 1999). Besides, such movements were largely not cultural sensitive and oriented towards prohibition of alcohol use. Corruption is the second reason where fine collected though the imposition of 'dry-zone' to those who violate the regulation is misused by Governmental officials. People complained that the first people who reintroduced alcohol in 'dry-zone' areas after the ban were the CDO, and district level leaders of political parties. Third, there is no strong legal status of such movements. Fourth, male-participation in such movement is minimal. Finally, it has increased the black-market for the distillery product across the 'dry-zone'. One of the examples of the failure of anti-alcohol movement is from Dasharath Municipality in Baitadi district.

Municipality Removes Ban on Alcohol

"Dasharath municipality has given permission to people to openly sell and distribute alcohol within the municipality area in violation of the ban on sale and distribution of alcohol in the Baitadi district imposed by the District Council.

The District Council had banned the sale and distribution of alcohol within the district six years ago to stop the social perversions that might take place in the society due to alcohol.

People who spearheaded the campaign to ban alcohol in 1994 say that the reversal of the ban was a sad thing. When the ban was in force, those who consumed alcohol were fined one thousand rupees and those who were engaged in brewing of alcohol were fined according to the amount they produced.

The municipality sources said the account of the amount earned due to fines was not properly maintained and the amount of alcohol consumption had not declined significantly with complicity of influential people in the society and senior civil servants and only poor people were fined if they consumed alcohol on the other. Therefore, they felt the compulsion that people should be allowed to sell alcohol openly in the municipality area." (The Kathmandu Post, August 23, 2000).

In our sample, one-third said that there was anti-alcohol campaign in their community. A complete prohibition of alcohol production and selling during the survey period was reported in our sample areas in Doti and Nuwakot districts. The former lies in far-western hills and the latter lies in central hills of Nepal. Two thirds of the respondents from Palpa (western hill) district reported that there was anti-alcohol campaign in their community. Similarly, at least 30 per cent of the total respondents from Kaski, Sindhuplanchok, Sarlahi, Rupandehi, and Dang reported that there was anti-alcohol campaign in their community.

Local level administration has also been taking initiative of anti-alcohol movement. One example is from Nuwakot district. It was declared dry-zone in the beginning of 1999. Initially, there were local groups such as mothers group and youth group who started anti-alcohol movement in some of the villages of the district. Realizing the adverse impact of alcohol use in the district, the Chief District Office announced Nuwakot as a dry-zone. The role of police is widely recognised.

Before announcing dry-zone in the district, alcohol was the main cause behind vandalism and domestic violence. In the village fairs and other gatherings, at least 8-10 alcohol induced violent cases came to the police. Similarly, it affected people's family life, men spent household income in drinks and beat their wives. In fact, it was suggested that alcohol was one of the reasons behind rampant girl trafficking in this region. People need money to drink and selling of girls provides easy income to unemployed people here.

Experience of Alcohol Free Zone, Nuwakot
A Police Officer recounts his experience in initiating alcohol free zone:

Inspiration from Women Groups
"Since I joined the police force, I have been to many districts, everywhere I found many of serious offences were alcohol induced. When I was in Sindhuli one year ago, I found that the local women's group had started anti-alcohol movement for some time. And there was a big conflict going on between anti-alcohol groups and alcohol entrepreneurs. The alcohol traders had finally won and the women's group was discouraged. It was when they approached me. I realized that it was necessary to exercise alcohol prohibition from the administration level."

Cultural Sensitive Programme

"Gurungs, Tamangs and Newars have their own faith and religion, we do not mean to interfere with that. We only mean to minimize excessiveness in the name of religion. During our campaign, we approached all the drinking groups, we discussed with them and provided them counseling. If you need to use alcohol in your rituals, use less, do not take it as an excuse to drink a whole bottle – that is our message. In this alcohol control campaign, its these drinking castes who are whole heartedly supporting our cause. If you go to villages like Lachyang, you will find Tamangs using alternative like milk and yogurt instead of alcohol in their rituals. If you make people aware about excessiveness in their own culture, they understand and they change. We should be self critical of our cultural practices if they are counter-productive."

Sustainability of Dry Zone

"In the question of sustainability, I will just say one thing - movement like this is not the responsibility of one single person, it should be the collective effort. One individual can only start it, people of the community should sustain it. That was the reason we have formed a 35-member supervision committee to supervise implementation of alcohol control measures. I believe a system has already been established, all people from different levels are making effort from their side, be it police, general public, VDC members or local clubs. The key is to ensure long-term sustainability by institutionalising it. "

In other places, there were several types of efforts undertaken to control alcohol in the community: prohibition and regulation of producing or selling of alcohol, public awareness, and counseling. Data indicate that prohibition was the major strategy for controlling alcohol in the community (Table 7.4). Women's group and police were reported to be the major agents of such campaigns. However, the impact of such campaigns is mixed in view of the respondents. Almost one-half regard its positive impact and the remaining one-half regard it is having no impact on controlling alcohol use in Nepal.

What has been their realisation about dry-zone, we asked women's groups in Nuwakot district. The responses to the anti-alcohol movement of Nuwakot district appear to be positive. People realized that there were less- fights and brawls during feast and festivals and less violence against women due to alcohol use in the community.

Table 7.4 Types of Effort Undertaken in the Community, Major Agents and Impact of Efforts

Activities	N	%
Effort		
No	1577	67.6
Yes	756	32.4
Total	2333	100.0
Types of Effort		
Prohibition	677	89.6
Public Awareness	55	7.3
Regulation	14	1.9
Education	10	1.3
Major Agents		
Women's Groups	423	56.0
Police	205	27.1
Local Clubs	66	8.7
NGOs/CBOs	45	6.0
Local Government	10	1.3
Others	7	0.9
Impact of such programme		
No impact	372	49.2
Positive impact	366	48.4
Negative impact	12	1.6
Don't Know	6	0.8
Total	756	100.0

The women felt safe, they said - "before dry zone, we had to hide when a drunk was coming, now they run away from us". The impact of alcohol prohibition on local economy is not clear but our key informants indicated that alcohol producers could shift their work to other income generating activities such as bee-keeping, goat farming, poultry etc. It does not, therefore, affect the livelihood of the poor alcohol producer. One of the negative impact of dry-zone was the emergence of black-market of alcohol.

Response to Dry Zone: Woman VDC Member from Tamang Community, Nuwakot

"Alcohol was declared prohibited in this area since last three months. The effort was initiated by District Superintendent of Police and Chief District Officer. After that, the change is visible, consumption level

has gone down by two third. Alcohol use has not stopped completely though, people continue to drink but not as much and not publicly. The status of alcohol free zone implies that people be punished if they are found drinking publicly.

The most striking change was during jatras (village fairs). Two main fairs in this district Devighat and Ghupche purnima were unusually hassle free this year. No fights, no brawls, people felt safe. If it is possible to control alcohol in such a massive public gathering, it is possible in small villages as well. VDCs too can be made completely alcohol free if the sellers are identified and proper action is taken.

We generally have the support of people in this effort, but those who are drinkers might not like it. They continue to drink and people continue to sell but in secret, not openly in shops. Since banning of alcohol, no shop is allowed to sell either local or distillery liquor. But the fact is people are making more money in the black-market since the ban because people are willing to pay more. A mana of Raksi previously priced Rs. 15 is sold for as much as Rs. 40. I asked a person why he is paying so much, he said what to do, I am addicted. The alcohol sellers are having a good time, the black market is exploiting the poor villagers. It is the poor who is always at the receiving end.

The alcohol sellers must be complaining now that they can not sell publicly. There are both middle class and lower classes involved in alcohol trade, mostly they are women. But I do not think banning alcohol has taken away their living, they can always do other things. People get into alcohol trade because it is easier way of earning money compared to working hard in the field or raising animals.

I come from drinking caste, but I support alcohol control completely. Granted that we need alcohol for our rituals and traditional purposes, we can still cut down on it, we can do by using less. People do not have enough to eat, yet they spent so much money on alcohol. The burden on women is worse, all their hard earned savings is spend by their men-folk in drinking instead of buying things for the household."

One of the successful alcohol reduction programme was launched by Jugal Community Development- a community based organisation and local partner of ActionAid working in Talamarang VDC of Sindhuplanchok district. Its target populations are the poor, women, children and *Dalits*. The themes of the activities are education, poverty reduction programmes, gender and micro finance. Under its micro finance, there were 17 groups, and a total of 107 members with majority of women. Its literacy programme is integrated with alcohol reduction campaigns, where women and children are aware of the adverse impact of excessive use of alcohol.

Majority of the people in the village comprise of Tamang - the traditional alcohol user groups. Jugal is trying to reduce the excessive use of alcohol particularly in feasts and festivals. The strategy is to allow alcohol use in their religion and culture occasions in a small amount and reduce the number of days of celebrations.

Alcohol Reduction Strategies: General Secretary, Jugal Community Development, Talamarang, Sindhuplanchok

> *"We do not have a direct programme against the use of alcohol, but we are addressing these issues indirectly. For example, in our "expense reduction and saving" programme, we urge the Tamang communities, who use alcohol liberally in their festivals and rituals, to cut down in amount. Our programme targets to make people aware about their own cultural practices that can be moderated. Similarly, we work with the community in spreading the knowledge about negative aspect of excessive alcohol use. We feel that alcohol use has gone down in places where we have directly reached with our programmes.*

> *We can not just tell people to stop drinking, people have to realise it themselves. For example they should realise production of alcohol directly affects food security. All alcohol products are made from food grains, millet is more used in this area. Among Tamang community, which is the majority in this area, almost 60 per cent of millet and maize production from farm is used in alcohol production. Compared to that, less amount of grain is used as food. Tamang people celebrate a 7-day ritual of Ghewa, each family spends Rs. 12-14 thousands on alcohol only. They have to organise much on unnecessary expense, and that can be controlled without completely doing away with the tradition. We have met with success in our cutting down expenses message. People have started organising two days of Ghewa instead of a week, and cutting down on the amount of alcohol served to the guest. Basically, we have met with success in this effort because we do not force people, we suggest them alternatives."*

7.2.3 Counterforces Perceived by Children Aged 10-17

This study also obtained information from children regarding the counter-forces of alcohol use as perceived by children. When children were asked whether the children be prevented from taking alcohol, overwhelming majority responded that they should be prevented (97.7%) (Table 7.3). It is almost 100 cent per cent for those from traditional non-users and is 96.3 per cent from traditional users. Children who reported to prevent using alcóhol were further asked how the use of alcohol be prevented. Among those who wanted to prevent, majority reported that educating people about negative impact of the use of alcohol is the best way to prevent alcohol use (47.8%). This is followed by those who suggest parents should control their children use of the alcohol (22.8%). Third important way of controlling the use of alcohol is by providing health awareness to people from harmful use of alcohol (11.8%). When it is seen cross-sectionally among traditional users and non-user groups, the pattern is found to be similar to the response of total respondents.

The information was also collected on the attitude of respondents for children to stop drugs and the way to stop it. The overwhelming majority (92.5%) reported that they want children who are using drugs to stop using drugs (Table 7.6).

Table 7.5 Perception of Respondents about Prevention of Alcohol

Description	Traditional users		Traditional non-users		Total	
	N	%	N	%	N	%
Whether children be prevented taking alcohol						
Yes	232	96.3	184	99.5	416	97.7
No	9	3.7	1	.5	10	2.3
Total	241	100.0	185	100.0	426	100.0
Way for prevention						
By educating	105	45.3	94	51.1	199	47.8
Health awareness	28	12.1	21	11.4	49	11.8
Controlling by parents	56	24.1	39	21.2	95	22.8
Awareness about harmful use	16	6.9	10	5.4	26	6.2
Adult not drinking in front of children	10	4.3	4	2.2	14	3.4
Not producing at home	10	4.3	14	7.6	24	5.8
Producing only on special occasion	5	2.2		-	5	1.2
Alcohol prohibition	2	.9	2	1.1	4	1.0
Total	232	100.0	184	100.0	416	100.0

Table 7.6 Attitude and Way to Stop Drug Use

Description	%	N
Attitude for children to stop drug use		
Yes	92.5	394
No	7.5	32
How to control drug use among children		
Prohibition of selling	11.0	47
Teaching about negative aspects	43.9	187
Not selling to children	2.3	10
Control by parents	14.3	61
Avoiding drug using companies	4.7	20
Providing love and care to children	3.1	13
Prohibition of production	4.9	21
Public awareness	7.7	33
Not providing children with money	0.5	2
Others	7.5	32
Total	100.0	426

They also provide way-out of how to stop using drugs. The majority of the children (43.9%) reported that the children have to be taught about negative aspects of drugs which hamper their lives, followed by those who want parents to control their children (14.3%). Prohibition of selling drugs (11.0%) is also an important drug control measure that the children perceived. Besides, public awareness, prohibition of production and making drug users isolated are also found to be important way to stop using drugs. Information collected from key informant interviews also suggests some strategies to control alcohol and drug use. The role of police, administration, NGOs, and international funding organisations is important to control the use of alcohol and drugs. They should be involved in campaigning and raising mass awareness. Families are another important stakeholder, which have contributing role in children using alcohol or drugs. They should give enough attention and become more accountable towards their children's well-being.

Chapter VIII

Summary and Conclusions

8.1 Summary

Utilizing both qualitative and quantitative, this study aimed at finding out the nature and extent of alcohol and drug use in Nepal in the socio-cultural and economic context. It examines the impact of such substances on children's life, and hence provides a viable ways for prevention through social action.

A total of 2,333 households from 16 districts were interviewed representing from rural-urban, ecological zones and development regions by including major ethnic groups. Target populations were adult members and children aged 10-17 years. From every fifth sample household, one child aged 10-17 were interviewed in order to understand the children's own perspectives on alcohol and drugs use. The total sample population was 13,526 of which 11,770 comprised of 6 years of age and above.

Regarding qualitative information, detail case history and key informant's interviews were conducted. Detail case histories were discussed from both users and non-users of alcohol, drugs and tobacco. Key informants were school teachers, police, health personnel, local elected leaders, social workers and women involving in anti-alcohol movements.

Of the sample population of 13,526, rural areas comprised of 63.5 per cent. Among the three ecological zones, Tarai comprised of 50.9 per cent. Majority (37.2%) constituted hill caste, followed by hill ethnic group (33.2%), Tarai ethnic group (10.1%) and low caste (7.6%). Hindus predominate the sample population (83%). Fifty-four per cent of the total sample population constitutes traditional alcohol users while the rest for traditional non-alcohol users. Only 3 in 10 sample population aged 6 and above were illiterate. The sample population is characterised by high fertility, high dependency ratio and low proportion of working age population.

8.1.1 Alcohol Economy in Nepal

In Nepal, alcohol is produced at home and at industry. Both national and multinational companies are involved in producing distilled and brewery products.

A total number of large, medium and small alcohol industries registered in Ministry of Industry, was 68 (36 distilleries, 8 breweries and 24 small-scale industries by 2000). The capacity of the alcohol production per year is 42,483,428 LP liters from medium and large-scale industries and 50,000,000 liters of beer from Breweries. The small-scale industries have reported their capacity of production in Rs. is 2,387,350,000. Alcohol revenue constitutes more than 50 per cent of the total excise duty and 6 per cent of the total national revenue.

Livelihood of the household is also associated with the production of alcohol in Nepal. The poorer the household, the more they produce alcohol at home for the purpose of selling. This holds true for traditional alcohol users in Nepal.

One third of the sample households were producing alcohol at their home. The highest proportion was in eastern region. Mostly alcohol is produced during the feasts and festivals. An overwhelming majority of the alcohol producers produces alcohol for family use as well as for sale to earn money. For example, data indicate that more than three-fifth of households run their livelihood by alcohol income. The per capita production of alcohol was 33 mana. Of which 8 mana are consumed and the rest is sold. The per capita income from alcohol was Rs. 32,700 per month.

8.1.2 Extent and Patterns of Alcohol Use Among Adults

The overall alcohol prevalence rate is 39 per cent with 47.8 per cent for males and 39 per cent for females. More than two-thirds of adult males ever experienced any type of alcohol, the comparable figure for adult females was 39 per cent. More females in rural areas than in urban areas drink alcohol. For example, 43 out of 100 rural females ever experienced alcohol as against 30 out of 100 in urban areas. In rural Nepal, most traditional alcohol users use alcohol especially *Jand* as part of food. Proportion of alcohol users is the highest in Kathmandu, followed by hills/mountain and the least in the Tarai.

The proportion of alcohol users increases from 19 per cent for the youngest age group (less than 17 years) to almost half for respondents with 35-44 age group, then it steadily declines with increasing age. This holds trues for both males and females. Almost 46 per cent of females belonging to traditional alcohol user category are currently using any type of alcohol while the comparable figure for females from non-traditional group is only 3 per cent.

More than one-third of females in rural areas are currently using alcohol as against three in ten in urban areas. Increasing education implies lower level of current use of alcohol. For example, more than one third of females with no education are currently drinking alcohol while it is only 6 per cent for females with SLC and above education.

Similarly, of the total respondents, 37.6 per cent are currently using the last 30 days of the survey. One in 10 adult members were found to be daily users.

Jand/Chhang, home-made *Raksi* and local *Raksi* are the most common drinks in Nepal. Almost 45 per cent of the total respondents have experienced beer, one third have experienced distillery products and less than one fifth have experienced foreign products. Access to alcohol market is largely available for males. In Nepal, females usually do not take alcohol in hotels and restaurants even if they are from traditional user group.

8.1.3 Context of Alcohol

About 57.6 per cent respondents have had hotel/restaurant/bars/shops. selling alcohol in their neighbourhood. About 54 per cent respondents were using alcohol at their home.

About one-fourth of the respondents reported that children start using alcohol when they enter the age of 16. A significant proportion (11%) reported that children start using alcohol by birth and 9 per cent reported at age 5-9 years and 9 per cent at age 10-15 years. Alcohol was considered as a problem when it becomes uncontrolled (24.6%), results in violence (19.7%) and it get started by children (13%).

Overall, three-fifth of the respondents usually take alcohol in particular type of occasion while the rest take alcohol even without special occasion. The latter type of alcohol users mostly come from traditional non-user families who do not drink for religious or cultural purposes.

Two-thirds of the respondents take alcohol at their own home, one-fifth at market and one-tenth at friend's place. However, the context of alcohol use widely differs by gender. An overwhelmingly majority of women take alcohol at their home (93.5%) and a few women take alcohol outside home.

The major reasons for taking alcohol were entertainment, as food and painkillers. Other reasons include 'medicine', 'problem solver', 'get energy', 'status symbol', and 'social lubricant'. More females than males take alcohol as food subsistence, as painkiller, and as medicine.

Almost all key-informants are concerned with religious and cultural values of alcohol use. Besides, political protection, lack of effective laws and ineffective implementation, open boarder, and easy access to alcohol are important reasons. They also blame the government fro not being serious to implement laws and regulations regarding the control of alcohol use because for the government it is one of the contributing sources of national revenue.

8.1.4 Drug Experience

On the average, prevalence of drugs is 2.7 per cent, 4.6 per cent for males and only 0.6 per cent for females. About 7 out of 100 respondents have ever experienced any type of drugs and about 10 males and 1 female out of 100 ever experienced any type of drugs.

Males predominate females by five-fold in taking drugs. The younger generation is more likely to have experienced drugs during the last 12 months as compared to the older generation. Cannabis appears to be the most common drugs in Nepal. Others are heroin, opiates, tranquilisers and glue.

Majority of drug users were getting drugs from friends and then from drug sellers. One of the sources of drugs was identified as cross-border supply from India. Public places, own homes, and friend's places were the common places of drug use. Similarly, majority of drug users take drugs with their friends. The major reason for drug use is their company and for entertainment, and a few reported that they were using drugs to forget their sorrow and as a medicine.

8.1.5 Impact on Children's Life

The overall prevalence of alcohol use among children aged 10-17 is 17.4 per cent for current use with 21.8 per cent for boys and 11.2 for girls. The most frequently used beverage by children are homebrews known as *Jand/Chaang* (91.9 per cent).

Age of children seems to be vital for using alcohol, drugs, and tobacco. Higher age is associated with higher use of substances.

Besides age and gender, education appears to be clearly associated with alcohol use, that is, increasing education means decreasing prevalence of alcohol.

A substantial proportion of children (9.2%) were using alcohol during the last 30 days. The proportion of children using alcohol decreases as the type shifts from more affordability to less affordability and from cheaper to expensive ones.

Our analysis indicates that use of alcohol, drugs, and tobacco is positively associated each other and alcohol use by children can be attributed to parents' use of alcohol, drugs, and tobacco.

Early childhood is affected by the use of substances, the median age of alcohol initiation was 13 years. This is usual because among traditional user communities, cultural and religious ceremonies and social gatherings are considered as a gateway of initiating alcohol use for both adults and children. Traditional and cultural occasions appear to be the most important occasion of initiating of alcohol (60% children initiate in these occasions). Initiation to alcohol is entirely related with our traditional and cultural rituals, while the initiation of drugs is a complex process. Availability of drugs has also made tremendous increase of drug users among young and children in urban areas of Nepal.

Adults see the major impacts of alcohol use on children's life as violence and physical abuse (33.4%), neglect and mental abuse (28.5%), deprived from education (20.2%) and children started to use alcohol (11.1%). Other impacts include malnutrition and children run away from home. Broadly, the impact of alcohol use on children's life can be categorised into social and economic impact on children's life.

Excessive use of alcohol often results in loss of wealth, which causes people to get into debt and poverty. Then, people can not afford children's schooling, leading to likelihood of children to drop out from school. This situation is associated with high magnitude of child labour scenario, especially worst forms, where children can be economically exploited, psychologically abused/neglected, physically tortured and socially manipulated for work not suited to their age and capacity.

Excessive use of alcohol is also linked to the economic exploitation in some communities of Nepal. One of our key informants from Nuwakot reported that most of the traditional alcohol user groups have lost their land due to excessive use of alcohol and the land has been mortgaged to the upper caste people, traditionally alcohol-non user groups.

Types of impact as perceived by children due to their parent's use of alcohol is examined and considerable proportion of children (29.4%) reported that the impact of parent's use of alcohol on children life exists. The reported impacts by children include mental abuse like neglect and scolding, physical abuse, malnutrition/ starvation, encouragement to use alcohol and no schooling.

The impact of drug use and/or trafficking on children is much intense than the impact by alcohol use on children's lives. Some of our key informants reported that their children were jailed for several months for drug abuse and peddling.

8.1.6 Counter-forces

This study identifies the counter-forces at three levels: at the national level, at the community level and at the household level. Laws and policies are at the top, anti-alcohol movement at the community in the middle and family members at the household level.

National Level Counter-forces

Several laws have been adopted regarding alcohol and drug use in Nepal. Among such laws are Alcohol Act, 2023, Alcohol Act, 2031, Hotel Regulations and the Sale and Distribution of Alcohol Act, 2023, National Broadcasting Act, 2049, Vehicle and Transport Regulation Act 2049, Local Administration Act, 2028 and Alcohol (First Amendment) Act, 2056. These acts, by and large, are concerned with the production, distribution and taxes of alcohol rather than reduction of harmful use of alcohol. Alcohol Act, 2056 is the one that prevents selling of alcohol to children aged below 16 years of old. Still it fails to charge the penalty to those who violate the law. In general, the main problem of such acts is the ineffective implementation and ineffective network system to operate the law. At the same time, there is no formal institution to co-ordinate the activities of different line ministries regarding the controlling and/or regulating alcohol.

Most laws are violated in every aspect of life. License provisions are weakening, hotel or restaurant's regulations are weakening due to lack of supervision and corruption, and print media are being attracted by good money from the alcohol producers. There is a business holders' pressure vis-à-vis politicians not to announce any dry-zone in the country.

Nepal has given a serious attention to drug control since the mid-seventies. At least 12 Acts have been adopted to control the illicit use of drugs in Nepal. At the central level, drug control policy exists. The goals are to enforce laws, reduce production, consumption and selling of drugs, build social support for drugs induced disabilities and provide treatment and rehabilitation including co-ordination with national and international organisation working against drug abuse.

Community and Household Level Counter-forces of Alcohol Use

This study deals with the counter-forces to the alcohol production, selling and consumption perceived by the respondent at two different levels: household level and community level. In Nepalese context, family is the basic unit of decision making in every aspect of life rather than individual. Any attempt to control or reduce alcohol consumption should focus on family and make them aware of the disadvantages of excessive use of alcohol.

Adult respondents do suggest to control and/or regulate alcohol use at their home only with control of production and selling, regulation and control of alcohol use, and raising awareness at the family. Majority of respondents were in favour of prohibition of alcohol production and selling (44%), followed by regulation of alcohol consumption. Similarly, one-fifth of the respondents stress the need to focus on family, especially head of the household.

In patriarchal society like Nepal, the role of men in controlling alcohol consumption still remains imperative at the household level. However, most of the anti-alcohol movements in Nepal are led by women and their role in controlling alcohol should not be minimised.

No national level anti-alcohol movement in Nepal has started yet. Local level anti-alcohol movements started by women first, then followed by CBOs, NGOs and Government agencies such as CDOs and DSPs office. Such movements largely fail because of the lack of proper legal status (alcohol not prohibited) under the law. Authorities can act only against the alcohol induced disturbances. However, upon the report of local people, the administration can act against certain social problems. In the anti-alcohol movement that started after the democracy, there was an extraordinary popularity and within a few years the movement spread from far-west to other parts of Nepal. Such movement passes through different phases: (i) populist initiation by women; (ii) taken over by the local government; (iii) news of positive impact; (iv) discontent among alcohol entrepreneurs (court cases against dry-zones); (v) revision of alcohol laws, state supporting alcohol distribution; (vi) alcohol sale reopen, indigenous products in market is replaced with distillery products and finally, news of social problems due to excessive alcohol use.

In our sample, one-third of the respondents knew about anti-alcohol campaign in their community. A complete prohibition of alcohol production and selling was reported in Doti, far-western and central hill districts. However, data do not provide information on the nature, extent, and the sustainability of such campaigns.

The major efforts undertaken to control alcohol in the community as reported by the respondents were prohibition and regulation of alcohol production and selling, public awareness, and counseling. In view of the respondents, impact of such efforts is dubious.

All the key informants emphasised the need of awareness programme for controlling and/or regulating alcohol and drugs. Other measures suggested to include the need for mass campaign, anti-alcohol movement, education, parent's attention to the children, and tight security in the open boarder between India and Nepal.

8.2 Conclusions

8.2.1 Alcohol

Two competing perspectives exist in dealing with the alcohol use in development literature. One perspective views alcohol through health concerns. The WHO is the yardstick in this perspective. The overall notion is to control the use of alcohol since it reduces the longevity of human life. Societies particularly those adhering to Protestant in America, Muslims everywhere, and Hindus in South Asia have such views about alcohol. They view that alcohol should be stigmatized as a drug and discouraged its use as strongly as possible. However, WHO in its recent report suggested that approaches to alcohol must be consistent with local cultures and mores. Each country must develop its own unique mix of strategies. Increased attention to alcohol and a commitment to implementing comprehensive programmes of education, treatment and regulation will help to reduce and avert an epidemic of alcohol-related disability, diseases and death worldwide (WHO, 1999).

Another perspective views alcohol as culture and lives. Hanson, an American Sociologist, and Heath, an American Anthropologist, are in the view that alcohol prohibition encourages undesired consequences in the society such as black-market, violence, and other social crimes. Control can not be achieved in a real sense. Their notion is to regulate the use of alcohol. Furthermore, they regard alcohol use in a continuum from the most harmful to the normal and sometimes beneficial one.

Heath (1990) emphasizes the need to take into account a wide variety of social, psychological, and physical benefits of moderate drinking that have been long recognized cross-culturally. He explains that the nature of problems that are associated with alcohol is a matter of social construction, negotiated differently by various constituencies, at various times. Putting problem drinkers and moderate drinkers in the same category is one mistake social scientists make and its implication is that it shall take away the focus from studying harmful drinking behaviour closely.

Previous studies[14] from Nepal were mainly directed towards prohibition approach with little attention to the cultural, religious and social values of alcohol in Nepal. They mostly relate alcohol use with the social crime and violence against women and children. Subba et al. (1995) have analysed alcohol and drug use in the socio-cultural and political perspective of the 'indigenous' people in Nepal who belong to traditionally alcohol-user group. This perspective associates alcohol and drug abuse and related delinquencies and deviant behaviour to poverty, deprivation, low level of education, social injustice, social isolation and cultural discrimination that are faced by people from ethnic groups who differ from the mainstream of dominant culture. The alcohol and drug prevention effort in such scenario should be made in the context of empowerment of the backward communities, their representation in the decision making, due share in country's resources, education and information in their language. A thorough understanding of the socio-cultural characteristics and psychographics of people should be established in order to design culturally appropriate programme for alcohol and drug prevention.

Our findings do indicate that regulation of alcohol consumption in consideration of different cultural norms is the best intervention approach for the reduction of excessive production, consumption and distribution of alcohol. The major conclusions of our study are the followings.

i. Alcohol Use a Common Phenomenon: Disappearing Religious and Cultural Barriers

---

[14] SAATHI (1997) found that alcohol abuse was the second biggest cause behind crime against women and girls. CWIN (1998) found 10 per cent of the violence against women are attributed to alcohol use by the spouse. Similarly, about 90 per cent of the road accidents are attributed to drunk driving (Dhital, 1999). Dhital (1999) found about 16 per cent of the children in Kathmandu left home due to alcohol use in the family. The major types of impact on children's lives are violence against children, torture, children themselves initiated to substance use, indebtedness and poverty due to alcohol use in the family.

The use of alcohol in Nepal has been existing in time immemorial. Nepalese society has been segmented into *Matwali*, traditional alcohol users, and *Tagadhari*, traditional alcohol non-user. Most ethnic groups including 'untouchables', so-called lower strata of Hindu hierarchical caste system- are the traditional users, whereas Brahmin, Chhetri and Thakuri, so called hindu high caste groups, are not considered as traditional users of alcohol. Traditional users are allowed to drink by virtue of birth while non-users are not. However, religious and cultural barriers to consume alcohol have almost disappeared these days.

Although there are more than 60 per cent of the population under the category of traditional alcohol users, the overall prevalence of alcohol is 39 per cent with about 48 per cent of males and 29 per cent of females. This means that not all but about 60 per cent of the traditional users use alcohol. There are also a significant number of alcohol users from traditional non-user groups (15%). It is remarkable that 40 per cent of the people from alcohol using groups reported not drinking alcohol.

Kathmandu is the place where the use of alcohol is highest in Nepal. It is because Kathmandu is the capital city alcohol sale is common Most young and children are affected by growing consumerism. Even the traditional non-users are exposed to the consumption of alcohol. Hills and mountains have high prevalence rate due to domination of traditional alcohol users. By religion, Kirant has the highest prevalence of alcohol, followed by Buddhist - both religious groups belong to traditional alcohol user groups. These people are mostly clustered in mountain and hills.

ii. A Conducive Socio-psychological Environment for Alcohol Market

Familial and socio-psychological factors susceptible to alcohol use should be the main concern of a prevention programme. Easy access to and availability of alcohol in the market need to be discouraged. This can be possible through efforts from both the national (effective law enforcement) and local levels (public pressure).

The most influencing factor for using alcohol is the surrounding environment. The more accessibility to the hotel/restaurants/bar with selling alcohol and the more people use alcohol in the society. Production of alcohol at home and use by the family members are also contributing factors for using alcohol. The favourable environment for alcohol at community and home level is basically due to cultural importance of alcohol in Nepalese society. Most religious and cultural/ritual functions, alcohol is the most coveted item to offer to Gods and ancestors. Offering alcohol is also the most culturally indoctirned custom while hosting guests and relatives. In addition, it is a social lubricant, which prompts socialisation and relaxation after hard day's work.

Even if the importance of alcohol is embedded in the fabric of culture and social lives of people, it becomes a problem many times. Different cultures have their own control system and definition of which drinking behaviour is not tolerated. Alcohol is perceived as problem when it becomes uncontrolled and violent. The problem would be more pronounced when people from non-drinking cultures use alcohol.

iii. Alcohol Prohibition Movements: Not Sustainable

Most anti-alcohol movements targeted to prohibition of alcohol are almost a failure and could not be sustained in the long period even in a small community. Such movements basically weaken their momentousness in the sense that they have revitalized the black-market for multi-national products and inhibited the home production from indigenous technology. They are also less sensitive to cultural and ritual aspects of majority of the people. Alcohol production is also closely associated with the livelihood of the poorest of the poor households on the one hand. On the other hand, it is closely associated with the deep cultural and ritual values of some segments of Nepalese society.

iv. A relatively Weak Agent for Countervailing Alcohol Use: Poor and Deprived Women

Prevention of alcohol use is a challenging issue not only in terms of its religious and cultural importance but also its economic contribution to the poorest of the poor households in Nepal. Our study suggests that it is the most backward ethnic group with rampant poverty that produces alcohol and sells in the neighbourhood or at the market. At the same time, women are the main producers. Alteration of such activities needs to be integrated with other income generating activities in the society.

Paradoxically, most anti-alcohol movements were started by women but largely ended up with little success due to poor legal status of such movements including the women's less power in the community and in the local Government. In a patriarchal society like Nepal, the role of men in controlling alcohol consumption still persists at the household level.

v. Alcohol Use: A Macro-economic Implication

Despite the crux of alcohol market in the national revenue, it has macro-economic implication in the long run. Excessive use of alcohol reduces the longevity of human populations-increasing morbidity leading to increase in the health cost on the one hand. On the other hand, it reduces the working hours which results in a reduction of per capita income and overall economic growth.

Increasing use of alcohol implies increasing production of alcohol. The production of alcohol has been increasing at both sides: industries - distilled and brewed, and indigenous technology - fermented. Alcohol production contributes more than 50 per cent of total excise duty and more than 6 per cent share of national revenue. Even though there are a number of laws and acts to control and minimize use of alcohol, they are not effective and government does not tend to control and stop producing alcohol. If the alcohol industries were closed a significant share of revenue would be lost by the nation. The production of alcohol at home by the indigenous technology, which are mostly located at the rural areas of Nepal, is invisible because it does not come into national account. However, production, selling, and use of this type of alcohol is even more contributing to the alcohol economy in the country. It is because local alcohol is affordable and accessible to more. Income from alcohol is contributing to family subsistence for more than three-fifth of the households. The per capita household production of *Jand/Chhang* and *Raksi* is about 17 liters per month for those involved in this business.

vi. Alcohol Use Has Negative Impact on Children's Life

A general observation on the impact of taking alcohol on children's life is the worsening of human capability such as health, education and income. There is a vicious cycle of such impact. When deprived children become parents, there is likely that their children would also be again unhealthy, uneducated and poor.

Our empirical evidence shows that a substantial proportion of children was taking alcohol from their early childhood. Majority of parents are unsure that whether their children would drink in the future. Parents are also able to identify the impact of alcohol taking on their children's life. The major impacts reported were violence and physical abuse, neglect and mental abuse, deprivation from education and children taking up alcohol habit. As a result, an overwhelmingly majority of the parents are in favour of prevention of children from using alcohol. Children themselves also recognize the problem of alcohol use by their adult family members.

vii. Increasing Capability of Women: A Panacea for Reducing the Excessive Use of Alcohol

Excessive use of alcohol is largely sex selective- males being the excessive users. While it is the females who suffer indirectly by the excessive use of alcohol. Women have to bear the maximum burden of economic crisis and violence in the family, and their children also have to face lack of food and educational opportunity. Our study indicates that increasing female's education implies lower level of current use of alcohol. At the same time, alcohol movements are largely led by women in Nepal. Providing education among females would, therefore, strengthen the anti-alcohol campaigns. Alcohol prevention programmes should, therefore, be integrated with gender development programmes.

vii. Reduction of Harmful Alcohol Use Requires a Cultural Sensitive Prevention Approach

A rapid social revolution is, therefore, needed to control and/or regulate alcohol and drugs use in Nepal. The constituents of such revolution are the constituents of prevention through social actions, not the prohibition and rehabilitation. Prevention of harmful use of substances should be given prime concern in designing the programmes. Such programmes need to be carefully designed in a way that would be culturally sensitive and responsive. At the same time, rehabilitation approach would be useful to those who are already intoxicated. A good example of prevention programme is Jugal Community Development's work in Sindhupalchowk district.

Prevention through social actions can be a launched in the areas where the problems are severe at first. Then, lessons learnt from such actions can be expected to be diffused to other strata of population as the effectiveness of such actions increases. The role of NGOs, CBOs, and women's organisation is vital in the context where the role of Government is squeezed due to the liberalisation of our economy since 1990s. It follows that it is the civil society, which can approach to the marginalized and disadvantage group. Government's role may be limited to maintaining laws and orders.

8.2.2 Drugs

Ganja is an indigenous form of cannabis, which has been used traditionally in Nepal for centuries. The *Shiva* sect of Hindu religion allows taking *Ganja*. The use of *Ganja* is very classical. It is regulated by social norms and does not create social problems in the traditional social structure of Nepal. The history of modern drug use began in 1960s, when the *Hippies* from the western world introduced them in Nepal. Then, the types of drugs gradually shifted from cannabis to synthetic opiates and sedatives-hypnotics, and their modes of administration also changed from smoking or ingesting to injecting (Chaterjee et al., 1996).

Despite several efforts have been made to control drug abuse by making a number of laws and acts and by a number of GOs and NGOs working against drug abuse in Nepal, the drug abuse has been increasing day by day. The government and social intervention against drug are not successful.

The overall prevalence of drugs is 2.7 per cent with 4.6 per cent for males and 0.6 per cent for females. The most prone area for drug abuse in Nepal is urban area for the synthetic drugs and central Tarai for the natural drugs (*Ganja*). Urban areas, especially Kathmandu,

Pokhara, and Dharan have been considerably exposed to western culture. The central Tarai is an area where a significant amount of *Ganja* has been produced.

The drug abuse is possibly high among those who are relatively better in terms of occupation, education, and residence. It is because they are relatively more exposed to everything. Younger generation is more likely to have experienced drugs. It is peer groups who begin using drugs in the name of entertainment and relief from sadness. Easy access from friends who have link with drug sellers and from drug sellers itself is another reason.

An important sign from this study is that effective rules and regulations and concomitant programmes against drugs can control the drug use in Nepal. Overwhelming majority wanted to stop drug use. The programmes must be education and public awareness against drugs, maintaining social environment, and finally prohibiting the use of drugs.

8.3 Further Research Issues

- It is still unclear why many anti-alcohol movements led by women are not sustainable. It is important to understand the people's perceptions towards alcohol use and its prohibition.
- Further research is needed to understand the contribution of alcohol in our economy and the clout that alcohol industry has.
- Much research is needed to understand the socio-cultural characteristics of alcohol in communities where alcohol is a part of life.
- Focussed studies need to be done among children and young people at different geographical, economic, cultural and social levels to understand fully how and to which degree alcohol and drug is affecting them nationally and globally.
- Much research is needed to understand whether the industry of alcohol or the traditional household production has greater impact on Nepalese society, particularly on children and women's life.
- Further research is recommended in a community where dry-zone is sustainable for a relatively longer time in order to clearly understand mechanisms and dynamics of successful programmes.

References Cited

Biswas, R. et al., 2000. "Early Onset Alcoholism in Nepal" in Abdul Khalid (ed.), *The Nepalese Journal of Psychiatry*, Vol. 1(2) (Kathmandu: Department of Psychiatry and Mental Hospital), pp.138-139.

Chatarjee et.al., 1996. *Drug Abuse in Nepal: A Rapid Assessment Study* (Kathmandu: New ERA).

Dhital, Rupa,1999. Alcohol and Children in Nepal, *Bal Sarokar,* Issue No. 35 (CWIN: Kathmandu), pp. 2-10.

_____, 1998. *Alcohol Use in Nepal*, paper presented at "Growing Consumption of Alcohol in Nepal: A Challenge", Organized by RECPHEC-Nepal (Kathmandu: RECPHEC-Nepal), 24-25 December 1998.

EUROCARE AND COFACE, 1998. *Alcohol Problems in the Family* (England: EUROCARE AND COFACE).

Heath, David, 2000. *Drinking Occasions, Comparative Perspectives on Alcohol and Culture* (Philadelphia: BRUNNER/MAZEL) pp.159-198.

Koirala, et al., 2000. "Alcohol Dependency in a Five Year Old Girl", in Abdul Khalid (ed.), *The Nepalese Journal of Psychiatry*, Vol. 1(2) (Kathmandu: Department of Psychiatry and Mental Hospital), pp.144-45.

Maskey, Mathura Prasad, 2000. "Shri Distillery is the First Company in the South Asia who received ISO-9002", *The Free Market*, A Fortnightly Magazine, Year 3, No. 3 (Kathmandu: Free Market), pp 40-41.

Ministry of Agriculture, 1996. *Agriculture Marketing Information Bulletin*, Special Issues (Kathmandu: Marketing Development Division, Department of Agriculture).

Ministry of Home Affairs, 1996. *Narcotics Control Bulletin,* Year 6, No.1 (Kathmandu: Narcotic Drug Control Division).

_____, 1998. *Narcotics Control Bulletin,* Year 8, No.1 (Kathmandu: Narcotic Drug Control Division).

_____, 1999. *Narcotics Control Bulletin*, Year 9, No.1 (Kathmandu: Narcotic Drug Control Division).

Mohan Davinder, and Sharma H.K., 1995. "India*", International Handbook on Alcohol and Culture*, in Dwight B. Heath (ed.) (London: Greenwood Press), pp. 128 –141.

Nepal South Asia Study Center, 1998. Nepal Human Development Report (Kathmandu: Nepal South Asia Study Center).

SAATHI, 1997. A Situation Analysis of Violence Against Women and Girls in Nepal (Kathmandu: The Asia Foundation).

Shah, Souvagya, 2000. "Alcohol, State and Women", *Himal,* Year 10, No. 13/14, October (Kathmandu: Himal), pp. 93-98.

Sinha U.K. et al., 2000. "Indirect Psychosocial Cost of Alcoholism: A Preliminary Analysis" in Abdul Khalid (ed.) *The Nepalese Journal of Psychiatry*, Vol. 1(2) (Kathmandu: Department of Psychiatry and Mental Hospital), pp.98-105.

Spotlight, 2000. *US Annual Narcotics Report on Nepal*. No. 34, March (Kathmandu: Spotlight).

Subba, Chaitnya et al.,1995. *Alcohol and Drug Abuse among Indigenous Population*, A proceeding of Symposium held in July 22-23 organised by DAPAN (Kathmandu: Drug Abuse Prevention Association Nepal).

Subedi, Lila Nath, 1999. *Alcohol Use and Its Impact* (Narayanghat: Chitwan Adhyan Kendra), pp. 73-77.

The Kathmandu Post, 2000. *Municipality Removes Ban on Alcohol,* 23 August (Kathmandu: The Kathmandu Post).

Vaidya TR et al., 1993. *Social History of Nepal* (New Delhi: Anmol Publications Pvt. Ltd.), pp.138 – 171.

WHO, 1999. *Global Status Report on Alcohol* (Geneva: World Health Organisation).

Appendices

Appendix: 1 Classification of Caste/Ethnicity in Nepal

Caste Group		Ethnic Group		Others
Hill Caste A	**Tarai Caste**	**Hill/mountain ethnic group**	**Tarai ethnic**	**Others**
Hill Brahmin	Marwadi	Limbu	Dhimal	Muslman
Chhetri	Paidar	Tamang	Tharu	Others
Gaine	Kahato	Magar	Mandal (Dhanuk)	
Giri	Yadav, Ahir, Ray	Gurung		
	Malha Sahani	Rai		
Hill Caste B	Bihari, Rauta, Kurmi	Newar		
Damai	Chamar, Mahra	Khadki		
Kami	Thakur, Barahi	Thakali		
Sarki	Kumhar (Pandit)	Chepang		
	Dhobi	Bhujel		
	Das, Mallik	Kumal		
	Gupta, Saha			
	Hajara			
	Dom, Paswan			
	Bada Sunar			
	Tarai Others			
	Kahar			
	Sahu			

Source: *Appendix 1, Article 2(b), Ministry of Local Development, His Majesty the Government and Gurung, Harka, 1995. Ethnic Demography in Nepal (Kathmandu: NEFAS).*

Appendix: 2 Classification of Alcohol User and Non-user by Tradition

Traditional user		Traditional Non-user	Unspecified
Limbu	Tharu	Chhetri	Hajara
Tamang	Malha Sahani	Hill Brahmin	Tarai Others
Magar	Mandal	Marwadi	
Gurung	(Dhanuk)	Yadav, Ahir, Ray	
Rai	Bihari, Rauta,	Thakur, Barahi	
Newar	Kurmi	Kumhar (Pandit)	
Damai	Chamar, Mahra	Dhobi	
Kami	Khadki	Muslman	
Sarki	Dom, Paswan	Das, Mallik	
Dhimal	Thakali	Gupta, Saha	
Paidar	Kumal	Giri	
Bhujel	Gaine	Bada Sunar	
Kahato	Kahar	Sahu	
	Chepang		

Source: These were identified based on discussion with Dr. Om Gurung, Anthropologist and key informants.

Appendix: 3 Legal Provisions Regarding Drugs Offences and Punishment in Nepal

Drugs	Offence	Degree	Imprisonment	Fine (in NRS)
Cannabis	abuse		Up to one month	Up to 2000
Cannabis	cultivation	Up to 25 plants	Up to 3 months	Up to 3000
Cannabis	cultivation	more than 25 plants	Up to 3 years	5000 to 25000
Cannabis	production	Up to 50 grams	Up to 3 months	Up to 3000
	manufactures	from 51-500 grams	1 month to 1 year	1000 to 5000
	trafficking	501 grams to 2 kg.	6 months to 2 years	2000 to 10000
	sales	2 kg to 10 kg.	1 to 3 years	5000 to 25000
	export/import	Above 10 kg.	2 to 10 years	15000 to 100000
Opium	abuse		Up to 1 year	Up to 10000
	cultivation	Up to 25 plants	1 to 3 years	5000 to 25000
	cultivation	more than 25 plants	3 to 10 years	25000 to 1000000
	export/import	Up to 25 grams	6 to 10 years	9000 to 25000
		25 to 100 grams	10 to 15 years	75000 to 200000
		more than 100 grams	15 years to life	500000 to 2000000
Any psychotropic substances prohibited by national gazette	Abuse, Trafficking, Smuggling, Cultivation, production		Up to 2 months	2000
			2 to 20 years	100000 to 2000000

Source: Ministry of Home Affairs, 1996.Ministry of Home Affairs, (1996). Narcotics Control Bulletin, Year 6 no 1. (Kathmandu: Narcotic Drugs Control Division).

APPENDICES

Appendix: 4 Drug Control Initiatives in Nepal

Description	Year
Liquor Control Act, 1960: This act made compulsory licensing to produce and sell Cannabis.	1960
Narcotic Drug (Control) Act, 1976: The Act banned the production, storage, sell, consumption, and trade of all types of narcotics and psychotropic substances listed in the Act.	1976
First Amendment of the Narcotic Drug (Control) Act, 1976: It made the provision to control certain morphine derivatives by prescription. This Act introduced the concept of controlled substance Act.	1981
Second Amendment of the Narcotic Drug (Control) Act, 1976: It made the provision of panelizing the physicians who violate the Act.	1987
HMG/Nepal became the party to the UN Single Convention on Narcotic Drugs 1961 as amended by the protocol of 1972.	1991
HMG/Nepal became party to 1988 UN Convention against Illicit Trafficking of Narcotic Drugs and Psychotropic Substances.	1991
Revision and third amendment of the Narcotic Drug (Control) Act, 1976.	1992
Bi-lateral agreement between UNDCP and HMG/N on the implementation of the Drug Abuse Control Master Plan in Nepal.	1992
A specialised Narcotic Drug Control Law Enforcement Unit (NDCLEU) as underlined in the Master Plan was established under the Narcotic Drug Control Division (NDCD), Ministry of Home Affairs.	1992
Drug Abuse Demand Reduction Project (DADRP) was established to look into matter related to demand reduction activities.	1994
Establishment of Inter-departmental co-ordination committee on precursor control (ICCPC) for effective control of precursor chemicals.	1998

Appendix: 5 Distilleries and breweries in Nepal as of May 2001

S.N	Name of Distillery	Address
1.	Jawalakhel Distillery	Jawalakhel
2.	Mahendra Sugar & General Enterprises	Bhairahawa
3.	General Liquors Pvt. Ltd.	Biratnagar
4.	The Nepal Distillery Pvt. Ltd.	Kathmandu
5.	Highland Distillery Pvt. Ltd.	Kathmandu
6.	Tribeni Distillery Pvt. Ltd.	Bhairahawa
7.	Triveni Distillery	Bhairahawa
8.	Shah Distillery Pvt. Ltd.	Nepalgunj
9.	Tri Shakti Distillery	Godavari
10.	Udaypur Distillery	Udaypur
11.	Birgunj Chini Karkhana	Parawanipur
12.	Shree Distillery Pvt. Ltd.	Nawalparasi
13.	Purbanchal Distillery Pvt. Ltd.	Sunsari
14.	Moonlight Distillery	Jhapa
15.	Dovan Ashbitra Pvt. Ltd.	Palpa
16.	Himali Distillery	Dharan
17.	Kaski Distillery	Kaski, Pokhara
18.	Chinnamasta Distillery	Dhanusha
19.	Rapti Distillery Pvt. Ltd.	Lamahi, Rapti
20.	Siddhababa Distillery	Rupandehi
21.	Snowland Distillery Pvt. Ltd.	Birgunj
22.	Bhawani Distillery	Bara, Simara
23.	Mount and Liquors	Kavre
24.	Amarawati Madhyashala Pvt. Ltd.	Sarlahi
25.	Ram Sugar Mills	Rautahat
26.	Rijal Tansi Industries Pvt. Ltd.	Sunsari
27.	Country Beer Udhyog Pvt. Ltd.	Dhading
28.	Dolkha Bhimsen Distillery	Dolkha
29.	Kaali Indistry Pvt. Ltd.	Kurintar, Chitwan
30.	Rainbow Distillery	Gorkha
31.	Rasua Distillery	Rasuwa
32.	Morang Sugar Mills	Morang
33.	Triyuga Distillery	Siraha
34.	New Everest Distillery	Siraha
35.	Baba Distillary Udhyog	Baswiti, Rautahat
36.	Shiva Distillary	Sankhuwasabha

37.	Gurans Distillary	Kapilvastu
38.	Himali Distillary	Tamaphof, Sankhuwasabha
39.	Shah Distillary	Sankhuwasabha
40.	Mohini Hygeine Products	Rupandehi
41.	Golden Globe Liquors	Biratnagar
42.	Bhusan Distillary	Biratnagar
43.	Himalayan Distillary Pvt. Ltd.	Parsa, Birgunj
44.	Lumbini Chini Karkhana	Bhairahawa
45.	Soubhagya Distillary	Siddharthanagar
46.	Shankar Distillary Pvt. Ltd.	Narayanghat
47.	Jyoti Distillary	Sankhuwasabha
48.	Sharda Distillary Pvt. Ltd.	Siraha
49.	Dhanusa Distillary Pvt. Ltd.	Basbiti, Dhanusa
50.	Sumi Distillary Pvt. Ltd.	Mukundapur, Nawalparasi
51.	Makalu Wine Industries Pvt. Ltd.	Sankhuwasabha
52.	Tukuche Distillary	Tukuche, Mustang
53.	Marfa Distillary Udhyog	Marfa, Mustang
54.	Rupandehi Distillary	Arunkhola, Nawalparasi
55.	Chandika Distillary Pvt. Ltd.	Morang
56.	Shree Ram Laxmi Distillary Udhyog	Marfa, Mustang

Breweries

1.	Gorkha Brewery	Nawalparasi
2.	Singha Brewery (Nepal) Pvt. Ltd.	Nawalparasi
3.	Mount Everest Brewery Pvt. Ltd.	Bharatpur
4.	United Brweweries Nepal Pvt. Ltd.	Hetauda Industrial Zone
5.	Himalayan Brewery Ltd.	Godavari, Lalitpur

Note: Information provided by VAT office, Tax department under Finance Ministry, 2001.